THE JOURNAL OF JOHN WESLEY

'I went at six to Turner's Hall which holds 2,000 persons. The press both within and without was very great. In the beginning of the expounding, there being a vault beneath, the main beam which supported the floor broke. The floor immediately sunk, which occasioned much noise and confusion. But, two or three days before, a man had filled the vault with hogsheads of tobacco, so that the floor, after sinking a foot or two, rested upon them, and I went on without interruption.'

In his *Journal*, John Wesley gives his readers a vivid – and sometimes amusing – picture of his life in eighteenth-century Britain and America. Wesley's account, originally written in code and later published in instalments, records the journeys of the man who travelled over 250,000 miles in the cause of the Christian gospel. Covering fifty-six years of his life, the *Journal* chronicles his open-air preaching, his inner doubts and conflicts, his journeys on horseback and by ship, and his encounters with many people – the famous, the infamous and the ordinary.

This new abridgement of Wesley's *Journal* has been made by Christopher Idle, Rector of the London parish of Limehouse. He has ministered in inner London since 1968. Married with four sons, he is also a student and writer of hymns. His fascination with John Wesley and George Whitefield, who both preached frequently in his present neighbourhood, goes back many years.

'The Christian faith will surely revive in this kingdom. You shall see it, though I shall not.'

The Rev. Samuel Wesley, father of John and Charles, near the time of his death in 1735

THE JOURNAL OF
John Wesley

ABRIDGED BY
CHRISTOPHER IDLE

A LION PAPERBACK
Tring · Batavia · Sydney

This abridgement copyright © 1986 Lion Publishing

Published by
Lion Publishing plc
Icknield Way, Tring, Herts, England
ISBN 0 85648 850 X
Lion Corporation
1705 Hubbard Avenue, Batavia, Illinois 60510, USA
ISBN 0 85648 850 X
Albatross Books Pty Ltd
PO Box 320, Sutherland, NSW 2232, Australia
ISBN 0 86760 684 3

First edition 1986
Reprinted 1986, 1987

Cover engraving of John Wesley © Mary Evans Picture Library

Printed and bound in Great Britain by
Cox and Wyman, Reading

CONTENTS

INTRODUCTION

In my study hangs a large picture of Oxford by moonlight. In the foreground stands John Wesley, welcoming young George Whitefield to the 'Holy Club'.

The reason for the picture is the reason for this book. I, an Anglican, have presumed to edit the Journals of the founder of Methodism, because like both these men I am a Church of England minister, a preacher of the gospel of Christ.

And while both these giants of evangelism were bigger than any labels, I owe a special debt to Douglas Wollen, Historian of Wesley's Chapel in City Road, whose former East London church was once a street away from mine. He first showed me the thrill in the very name 'Methodist'.

The thrill has sometimes faded where the fires burn low. But what fires they were – those Oxford lamps were to illuminate the world! If only the harmony in my picture could have been unbroken! And while the Wesleys led the way here (younger brother Charles being 'the first Methodist'), in conversion, field-preaching and initiatives in Bristol and London, Whitefield was the pioneer. With thirteen Atlantic crossings to Wesley's two, he may also have been first in exclaiming, 'the world is my parish!'

For most of that amazing century, Whitefield, the younger man, was seen as leader. It is said he was the greater preacher; on departing for America in 1739 he handed to Wesley a movement thirty thousand strong. The later eclipse in Whitefield's fame is balanced by the rise in Wesley's. John lived longer than George, organized better, and unremittingly propagated his own views.

The *Journal* is a case in point. Almost nothing survives from Whitefield's maturer years, but Wesley published instalments throughout his life. In hating slavery on the one hand, and certain kinds of privilege on the other, Wesley was more liberated than Whitefield from bondage to his generation. If both were children of their time, the wonder is how often, how gloriously, they were set free.

These selections show the bondage and the freedom. We take some of Wesley's bolder assertions (numbers, opinions, motives, details) with a pinch of salt; his unilateral claims and his tactical silences sometimes need the comment of another. In this abridgement, therefore, I have introduced many of the *Journal*'s fifty-six years with an observation from one of Wesley's contemporaries. This allows a different voice to break in on the devastating monologue. Often the extra quotation is his own, and sometimes it adds to the puzzle. Not every addition is a correction.

If it seems scandalous to reduce Wesley's story to less than a tenth of what he recorded, I can appeal only to his own example. 'I abridged Dr Watts' pretty *Treatise on the Passions*,' says a characteristic note; 'His hundred and seventy pages will make a useful tract of four and twenty.'

I have kept his exact words except where the calendar is clarified, corrected, or put in uniform style. Some names are inserted from initials or other evidence. No vital group of entries has been intentionally left out; but he was a great list-maker, and some of these numbered catalogues of names or reasons have gone. So have many long letters (his own or others') and several involved case-histories which cannot fairly be shortened. The Latin has almost disappeared; many landmarks of 'the people called Methodists' remain, but inevitably the travel-diary becomes a switchback rather than a carefully-planned itinerary. For a full picture of the unrivalled and almost uninterrupted journeyings, as for much else, the full account is needed.

One of many items borrowed, adapted, and perfected by Wesley for his own use was the system of shorthand which helps to explain how he wrote so fully in an already full programme. Praying, preaching, reading, riding, suffering, and organizing were his daily meat and drink. A typical early entry in his diary-notebook reads in manuscript: '8 re c ap p s h s c 1 2 3 4 p t b x ...' Stanley Ayling, in his book *John Wesley*, interprets:

'At eight a.m. read chapter appointed; prayed, sang a hymn; said the Creed, and Collects 1,2,3 and 4; Tate and Brady's metrical version of the Psalms; expounded …' Some of his developed codes are far more complex; he abbreviated for privacy as well as speed.

The secret diaries, as well as some lost or unpublished fragments of the full *Journal*, remind us of another crucial fact. In these pages we are not eavesdropping on the inner thoughts of a great man; many of these, mercifully, we shall never know. We see here what John Wesley wanted us to see. He has long pondered his words since their first hasty jotting down. He has prepared them for the printer, and edited them as carefully as any of the multitude of pages he ever published. If his reputation stands, or slips, on the *Journal*, that was his choice. The judgements expressed on friends and foes, books and places, churches and nations, varying between the exact and the absurd – these are what he would have us hear. In many ways, Wesley was 'his own Boswell'.

And some of the most tantalizing gaps are all his own. Among so many deaths, there is no account of the passing of his beloved Charles; the later tribute seems lukewarm enough. For different reasons he makes no reference, at the time, to his wedding – let alone the wedding that so nearly was, to Grace Murray in 1749. Let alone the tragi-comedy of Sophia Hopkey in Georgia years before. The decisive 'ordination' of Thomas Coke in 1784 (effectively claiming 'bishop' status for Wesley) goes unrecorded; we have to read the entry for 1 September 1784 very carefully indeed, since sometimes the plain-speaking of which he often boasted failed even this paragon of frankness.

The text of this abridgement is based on Nathanael Curnock's eight-volume *Standard Edition*, published by Charles H. Kelly 1909 - 1916. Some spellings are modernized in line with most editions. I have generally avoided the use of dots to indicate omissions, as they would constantly interrupt the flow of the story, and so some punctuation has been revised. However abbreviated, the vigour of Wesley's prose lives on; his style, itself no mean literary achievement, flashes and sparkles on every page, through every year. Love him or hate him – and most have loved him – God has blessed him, and his readers.

Facsimile of the first page of Wesley's Voyage Diary. This page covers 17, 18 and 19 October 1735.

WESLEY'S EARLY
YEARS

Wesley's boyhood: his mother's account

John Wesley included two letters from his mother, Mrs Susannah Wesley, in his *Journal*, at the account of her death in 1742. They describe home during John's early years. The first was written to John's father, the Rev. Samuel Wesley; the second was to John.

6 February 1712

As I am a woman, so I am also mistress of a large family. And though the superior charge of the souls contained in it lies upon you, yet, in your absence, I cannot but look upon every soul you leave under my care as a talent committed to me under a trust by the great Lord of all the families both of heaven and earth...

I resolved to begin with my own children, in which I observe the following method: I take such a proportion of time as I can spare every night to discourse with each child apart. On Monday I talk with Molly; on Tuesday with Hetty; Wednesday with Nancy; Thursday with Jacky; Friday with Patty; Saturday with Charles; and with Emily and Suky together on Sunday.

With those few neighbours that then came to me I discoursed more freely and affectionately. I chose the best and most awakening sermons that we have. Our company increased every night; for I dare deny none that ask admittance. Last Sunday, I believe, we had above two hundred. And yet many went away, for want of room to stand.

I cannot conceive why any should reflect upon you because your wife endeavours to draw people to church. For my part I value no censure upon this account. I have long since shook hands with the world.

As to its looking particular, I grant it does. And so does almost anything that is serious, or that may any way advance the glory of God or the salvation of souls.

As for your proposal of letting some other person read: alas! you do not consider what a people these are. I do not think one man among them could read a sermon without spelling a good part of it. Nor has any of our family a voice strong enough to be heard by such a number of people.

24 July 1732

Dear Son,

According to your desire, I have collected the principal rules I observed in educating my family. The children were always put into a regular method of living, in such things as they were capable of, from their birth: as in dressing, undressing, changing their linen, etc.

When turned a year old (and some before), they were taught to fear the rod, and to cry softly; by which means they escaped the abundance of correction they might otherwise have had, and that most odious noise of the crying of children was rarely heard in the house.

As soon as they were grown pretty strong, they were confined to three meals a day. At dinner their little table and chairs were set by ours, where they could be overlooked; and they were suffered to eat and drink (small beer) as much as they would; but not to call for anything. If they wanted aught they used to whisper to the maid which attended them, who came and spoke to me; and as soon as they could handle a knife and fork, they were set to our table. They were never suffered to choose their meat, but always made eat such things as were provided for the family.

Drinking or eating between meals was never allowed, unless in case of sickness, which seldom happened. Nor were they suffered to go into the kitchen to ask anything of the servants when they were at meat; if it was known they did, they were certainly beat, and the servants severely reprimanded.

At six, as soon as family prayers were over, they had their supper; at seven the maid washed them; and, beginning at the youngest, she undressed and got them all to bed by eight; at which time she left them in their several rooms awake – for there was no such thing allowed of in our house as sitting by a child till it fell asleep.

In order to form the minds of children, the first thing to be done is to conquer their will, and bring them to an obedient temper. To inform the understanding is a work of time, and must with children proceed by slow degrees as they are able to bear it; but the subjecting the will is a thing that must be done at once, and the sooner the better.

No wilful transgression ought ever to be forgiven children without chastisement, less or more, as the nature and circumstances of the offence require. I insist upon conquering the will of children betimes, because this is the only strong and rational foundation of a religious education.

The children were taught, as soon as they could speak, the Lord's Prayer, which they were made to say at rising and at bed-time constantly; to which, as they grew bigger, were added a short prayer for their parents, and some collects; a short catechism, and some portions of Scripture, as their memories could bear.

They were very early made to distinguish the Sabbath from other days, to understand they might have nothing they cried for, and to speak handsomely for what they wanted.

Every one was kept close to their business, for the six hours of school: and it is almost incredible what a child may be taught in a quarter of a year, by a vigorous application, if it have but tolerable capacity and good health.

For some years we went on very well. Never were children in better order, till that fatal dispersion of them, after the fire, into several families. In these they were left at full liberty to converse with servants and to run abroad, and play with any children, good or bad. They soon got knowledge of several songs and bad things, which before they had no notion of.

When the house was rebuilt, and the children all brought home, we entered upon a strict reform; and then was begun the custom of singing psalms at beginning and leaving school, morning and evening.

There were several by-laws observed. That no girl be taught to work till she can read very well, for the putting children to learn sewing before they can read perfectly is the very reason why so few women can read fit to be heard, and never to be well understood...

Wesley at school and college: his religion

This extract is taken from the *Journal* written at the time of his conversion. He describes his childhood 'till I was about ten years old' as a period of keeping rules without any idea of inward holiness, and continues:

The next six or seven years were spent at school; where, outward restraints being removed, I was much more negligent than before, even of outward duties, and almost continually guilty of outward sins, which I knew to be such, though they were not scandalous in the eye of the world. However, I still read the Scriptures, and said my prayers morning and evening. And what I now hoped to be saved by, was, (1) not being so bad as other people; (2) having still a kindness for religion; and (3) reading the Bible, going to church, and saying my prayers.

Being removed to the University for five years, I still said my prayers both in public and in private, and read, with the Scriptures, several other books of religion. Yet I had not all this while so much as a notion of holiness. I cannot well tell what I hoped to be saved by now, unless by those transient fits of what many divines taught me to call repentance.

When I was about twenty-two, my father pressed me to enter into holy orders. At the same time, the providence of God directing me to Kempis's *Christian Pattern*, I began to see, that true religion was seated in the heart. I was, however, very angry at Kempis for being too strict. I set apart an hour or two for religious retirement. I communicated every week. I began to aim at, and pray for, inward holiness. So that now, 'doing so much, and living so good a life', I doubted not but I was a good Christian.

Removing soon after to [Lincoln] College I applied myself closer to study. I advised others to be more religious. Meeting with Mr Law's *Christian Perfection* and *Serious Call*, although I was much offended at many parts of both, yet they convinced me more than ever of the exceeding height and breadth and depth of the love of God. And by my continued endeavour to keep his whole law, inward and outward, to the utmost of my power, I was persuaded that I should be accepted of him.

In 1730 I began visiting the prisons...

Wesley at Oxford: the 'Holy Club'

From John's letter to Mr Richard Morgan of Dublin, 18 October 1732:

In November 1729, at which time I came to reside at Oxford, your son, my brother, myself, and one more agreed to spend three or four evenings in a week together. Our design was to read over the classics, which we had before read in private, on common nights, and on Sunday some book in divinity. In the summer following, Mr Morgan told me he had called at the jail, to see a man who was condemned for killing his wife; and that, from the talk he had with one of the debtors, he verily believed it would do much good if any one would be at the pains of now and then speaking with them. This he so frequently repeated, that on the 24th of August, 1730, my brother and I walked with him to the Castle.

We were so well satisfied with our conversation there, that we agreed to go thither once or twice a week; which we had not done long, before he desired me to go with him to see a poor woman in the town who was sick. In this employment too, we believed it would be worth while to spend an hour or two in a week; provided the minister of the parish in which any such person was were not against it. But that we might not depend wholly on our own judgements, I wrote an account to my father of our whole design.

Soon after, a gentleman of Merton College, who was one of our little company, which now consisted of five persons, acquainted us that he had been much rallied the day before for being a member of *The Holy Club*; and that it was become a common topic of mirth at his college.

We still continued to meet together; and to confirm one another, as well as we could, in our resolutions; to communicate as often as we had opportunity (which is here once a week); and to do what service we could to our acquaintance, the prisoners, and two or three poor families.

To these we have added the observing the fasts of the Church; the general neglect of which we can by no means apprehend to be a lawful excuse for neglecting them. As for the names of

Methodists and so on, with which some of our neighbours are pleased to compliment us, we do not conceive ourselves to be under any obligation to regard them, much less to take them for arguments.

Wesley's doctrine: perfect love
From a letter 'to a friend': Londonderry, 14 May 1765:

In 1725 I met with Bishop Taylor's *Rules of Holy Living and Dying*. I was struck particularly with the chapter upon *intention*, and felt a fixed intention 'to give myself up to God', to give God all my heart. I sought after it from that hour.

In 1730 I began to be *homo unius libri* [a man of one book], to study (comparatively) no book but the Bible. I then saw, in a stronger light than ever before, that only one thing is needful, even faith that worketh by the love of God and man, all inward and outward holiness; and I groaned to love God with all my heart, and to serve him with all my strength.

1 January 1733, I preached the sermon on the Circumcision of the Heart, which contains all that I now teach concerning salvation from all sin, and loving God with an undivided heart. This was then, as it is now, my idea of Perfection.

Wesley's Diary and Journal: their beginnings
From the Preface to the first printed extract, the *American Journal*, published in Bristol, 1739:

It was in pursuance of an advice given by Bishop Taylor, in his *Rules for Holy Living and Dying*, that about fifteen years ago I began to take a more exact account of the manner wherein I spent my time, writing down how I had employed every hour.

This I continued to do till the time of my leaving England. The variety of scenes which I then passed through induced me to transcribe, from time to time, the more material parts of my diary, adding here and there such little reflections as occurred to my mind. Of this Journal thus occasionally compiled, the following is a short extract.

THE JOURNAL
1735 - 1790

1735

'My chief motive, to which all the rest are subordinate, is the hope of saving my own soul.'

John Wesley, letter to Dr John Burton of SPCK, on his reasons for going to Georgia; 10 October 1735

Tuesday, 14 October – Mr Benjamin Ingham, of Queen's College, Oxford, Mr Charles Delamotte, son of a merchant, in London, who had offered himself some days before, my brother Charles Wesley and myself, took boat for Gravesend, in order to embark for Georgia. Our end in leaving our native country was not to avoid want, God having given us plenty of temporal blessings, nor to gain riches or honour, but singly this – to save our souls, to live wholly to the glory of God. About four in the afternoon we found the *Simmonds* off Gravesend, and immediately went on board.

Friday, 17 October – I began to learn German, in order to converse with the Moravians, six-and-twenty of whom we have on board.

Sunday, 19 October – The weather being fair and calm, we had the morning service on quarter-deck. I now first preached extempore, and then administered the Lord's Supper to six or seven communicants. A little flock. May God increase it!

Monday, 20 October – Believing the denying ourselves, even in the smallest instances, might, by the blessing of God, be helpful to us, we wholly left off the use of flesh and wine, and confined ourselves to vegetable food, chiefly rice and biscuit.

Tuesday, 21 October – We sailed from Gravesend. Our common way of living was this: From four in the morning till five each of us used private prayer. From five to seven we read the Bible together. At seven we breakfasted. At eight were the public prayers, at which were present usually between thirty or forty of our eighty passengers. From nine to twelve I commonly learned German, and Mr Delamotte Greek. My brother writ sermons, and Mr Ingham instructed the children. At twelve we met to give an account to one another what we had done since our last meeting, and what we designed to do before our next. About one we dined. The time from dinner to four we spent with the people partly in public reading, partly in speaking to them severally, as need required. At four were the evening prayers. From five to six we again used private prayer. From six to seven I read in our cabin to two or three of the passengers, and each of my brethren to a few more in theirs. At seven I joined with the Germans in their public service. At eight we met again, to exhort and instruct one another. Between nine and ten we went to bed, where neither the roaring of the sea nor the motion of the ship could take away the refreshing sleep which God gave us.

Friday, 24 October – Having a rolling sea, most of the passengers found the effects of it. Mr Delamotte was exceeding sick for several days; Mr Ingham for about half an hour. My brother's head ached much.

Friday, 31 October – We sailed out of the Downs. At eleven at night I was waked by a great noise. I soon found there was no danger. But the bare apprehension of it gave me a lively conviction what manner of men ought those to be who are every moment on the brink of eternity.

Thursday, 20 November – The continuance of the contrary winds gave my brother an opportunity of complying with the desire of the minister of Cowes, and preaching there three or four times. The poor people flocked together in great numbers, and appeared extremely affected. We distributed a few little books among the more serious of them.

Sunday, 23 November – At night I was awaked by the tossing of the ship and roaring of the wind, and plainly showed I was unfit, for I was unwilling, to die.

Tuesday, 2 December –I had much satisfaction in conversing with one that was very ill and very serious, but in a few days she recovered from her sickness and her seriousness together.

Wednesday, 10 December – We sailed from Cowes, and in the afternoon passed the Needles. Here the ragged rocks, with the waves dashing and foaming at the foot of them, and the white side of the island rising to such a height, perpendicular from the beach, gave a strong idea of him that spanneth the heavens, and holdeth the waters in the hollow of his hand.

Saturday, 27 December – I endeavoured to reconcile Mrs Moore and Mrs Lawley with Mrs Hawkins, with whom they had had a sharp quarrel. I thought it was effected; but the next day showed the contrary.

1736

'My brother ... who was born for the benefit of knaves.'
Charles Wesley, *Journal*, 27 August 1736

Thursday, 1 January – Oh may the New Year bring a new heart and a new life to all those who seek the Lord God of their fathers!

Thursday, 15 January – Complaint being made to Mr Oglethorpe of the unequal distribution of the water among the passengers, he appointed new officers to take charge of it. At this the old ones and their friends were highly exasperated against us, to whom they imputed the change.

Saturday, 17 January – Many people were very impatient at the contrary wind. At seven in the evening they were quieted by a storm. About nine the sea broke over us from stem to stern; burst through the windows of the state cabin, where three or four of us were sitting. A bureau sheltered me from the main shock. About eleven I lay down and in a short time fell asleep, though very uncertain whether I should awake alive, and most ashamed of my unwillingness to die.

Sunday, 25 January – At seven I went to the Germans. I had long before observed the great seriousness of their behaviour. Of their humility they had given a continual proof, by performing those servile offices for the other passengers which none of the English would undertake. And every day had given them occasion of showing a meekness which no injury could move. If they were pushed, struck, or thrown down, they rose again and went away; but no complaint was found in their mouth. There was now an opportunity of trying whether they were delivered from the spirit of fear, as well as from that of pride, anger, and revenge. In the midst of the psalm the sea broke over, split the mainsail in pieces, and poured in between the decks, as if the great deep had already swallowed us up. A terrible screaming began among the English. The Germans calmly sang on. I asked one of them afterwards, 'Was you not afraid?' He answered, 'I thank God, no.'

Friday, 30 January – We had another storm, which did us no other harm than splitting the foresail. Our bed being wet, I laid me down on the floor and slept sound till morning.

Sunday, 1 February – We spoke with a ship of Carolina, and came within soundings.

Wednesday, 4 February – About noon the trees of Georgia were visible from the mast.

Thursday, 5 February – Between two and three in the afternoon God brought us all safe into the Savannah river.

Friday, 6 February – About eight in the morning I first set my foot on American ground. It was a small uninhabited island; Mr Oglethorpe led us to a rising ground, where we all kneeled down to give thanks. He then took boat for Savannah. When the rest of the people were come on shore, we called our little flock together to prayers. Several parts of the Second Lesson (Mark 6) were wonderfully suited to the occasion; in particular, our Lord's directions to the first preachers of his gospel, and their toiling at sea and deliverance – with these comfortable words: 'It is I, be not afraid.'

Saturday, 7 February – Mr Oglethorpe returned with Mr Spangenberg, one of the Moravian pastors.

Sunday, 8 February – I asked Mr Spangenberg's advice with regard to myself. He told me he could say nothing till he had asked me two or three questions. 'Do you know yourself? Have you the witness within yourself? Does the Spirit of God bear witness with your spirit that you are a child of God?' I was surprised, and knew not what to answer. He observed it, and asked, 'Do you know Jesus Christ?' I paused, and said, 'I know he is the Saviour of the world.' 'True,' replied he; 'but do you know he has saved you?' I answered, 'I hope he has died to save me.' He only added, 'Do you know yourself?' I said, 'I do.' But I fear they were vain words.

Friday, 13 February – We received information that Tomo-chachi and his Beloved Men were coming to see us. They sent us down a side of venison before them. In our course of reading to-day were these words: 'Yea, many people and strong nations shall come to seek the Lord of hosts in Jerusalem.'

Saturday, 14 February – About one Tomo-chachi, his nephew Thleeanouhee, his wife Sinauky, with two of their chief women, and three of their children, came on board. Sinauky brought us a jar of milk, and another of honey. As soon as we came in they all rose and shook us by the hand. Tomo-chachi spake by his interpreter, one Mrs Musgrove, to this effect:

'I am glad you are come. When I was in England, I desired that some would speak the Great Word to me; and my nation then desired to hear it. But we would not be made Christians as the Spaniards make Christians: we would be taught before we are baptized.'

Thursday, 19 February – My brother and I took boat, and, passing by Savannah, went to pay our first visit in America to the poor Heathens. But neither Tomo-chachi nor Sinauky was at home.

Sunday, 22 February – Mary Welch, aged eleven days, was baptized according to the custom of the first Church, and the rule of the Church of England, by immersion. The child was ill then, but recovered from that hour.

Wednesday, 25 February – [Savannah] Mr Delamotte and I took up our lodging with the Germans. They were always employed, always cheerful and in good humour with one another; they had put away all anger, and strife and clamour, and evil-speaking; they adorned the gospel of our Lord in all things.

Saturday, 28 February – After several hours spent in conference and prayer, they proceeded to the election and ordination of a bishop. The great simplicity, as well as solemnity, of the whole, almost made me forget the seventeen hundred years between, and imagine myself in one of those assemblies where Paul the tent-maker or Peter the fisherman presided, yet with the demonstration of the Spirit and of power.

Sunday, 29 February – We were refreshed by several letters from England.

Sunday, 7 March – I entered upon my ministry at Savannah. In the Second Lesson (Luke 18) was our Lord's prediction of the treatment which he himself (and consequently his followers) was to meet with from the world. Yet, notwithstanding these plain declarations of our Lord, notwithstanding my own repeated experience, I do here bear witness against myself, that when I saw the number of people crowding into the church, the deep attention with which they received the word, I could hardly believe that the far greater part of this attentive, serious people would hereafter trample under foot that word, and say all manner of evil falsely of him that spake it.

Sunday, 4 April – About four in the afternoon I set out for Frederica in a periagua – a sort of flat-bottomed barge. The next evening we anchored near Skidoway Island. I wrapped myself up from head to foot in a large cloak, to keep off the sand-flies, and lay down on the quarter-deck. Between one and two I waked under water, being so fast asleep that I did not find where I was till my mouth was full of it. I swam round to the other side of the periagua, where a boat was tied, and climbed up by the rope without any hurt more than wetting my clothes. 'Thou art the Lord by whom we escape death.'

Saturday, 17 April – Not finding, as yet, any door open for the pursuing our main design, we considered in what manner we might be most useful to the little flock at Savannah. And we agreed (1) to advise the more serious among them to form themselves into a sort of little society, and to meet once or twice a week, in order to reprove, instruct, and exhort one another. (2) To select out of these a smaller number for a more intimate union with each other, which might be forwarded, partly by our conversing singly with each, and partly by inviting them all together to our house.

Wednesday, 5 May – I was asked to baptize a child of Mr Parker's, second Bailiff of Savannah; but Mrs Parker told me, 'Neither Mr Parker nor I will consent to its being dipped.' I answered, 'If you "certify that" your "child is weak, it will suffice" (the rubric says) "to pour water upon it."' She replied, 'Nay, the child is not weak; but I am resolved it shall not be dipped.' This argument I could not confute. So I went home, and the child was baptized by another person.

Thursday, 3 June – [Frederica] Being Ascension Day, we had Holy Communion; but only Mr Hird's family joined with us in it. One reason why there were no more was, because a few words which a woman had inadvertently spoken had set almost all the town in a flame. Alas! how shall a city stand that is thus divided against itself; where there is envy, malice, revenge, suspicion, evil speaking, without end?

Thursday, 17 June – An officer of a man-of-war, walking just behind us, cursed and swore exceedingly; but upon my reproving him, seemed much moved, and gave me many thanks.

Saturday, 19 June – Mr Oglethorpe returned from the south, and gave orders on Sunday, the 20th, that none should profane the day by fishing or fowling upon it. In the afternoon I summed up what I had seen or heard at Frederica inconsistent with Christianity, and, consequently, with the prosperity of the place. The event was as it ought; some of the hearers were profited, and the rest deeply offended.

Tuesday, 22 June – Observing much coldness in Mr Horton's behaviour, I asked him the reason of it. He answered, 'I like nothing you do. All your sermons are satires upon particular persons, therefore I will never hear you more. And then your private behaviour – all the quarrels that have been here since you came have been 'long of you. And so you may preach long enough; but nobody will come to hear you.'

He was too warm for hearing an answer. So I had nothing to do but to thank him for his openness, and walk away.

Wednesday, 30 June – [Savannah] I hoped a door was opened for going up immediately to the Choctaws, the least polished, that is, the least corrupted, of all the Indian nations. But upon my informing Mr Oglethorpe of our design, he objected, not only the danger of being intercepted, or killed by the French there; but much more, the inexpediency of leaving Savannah destitute of a minister.

Thursday, 1 July – The Indians had an audience; and another on Saturday, when Chicali, their head man, dined with Mr Oglethorpe. After dinner, I asked the grey-headed old man what he thought he was made for. He said, 'He that is above knows what he made us for. We know nothing. We are in the dark. But white men know much. And yet white men build great houses, as if they were to live for ever.' I told him, 'If red men will learn the good book, they may know as much as white men.'

Hearing the younger of the Miss Boveys was not well, I called upon them this evening. I found she had only the prickly heat, a sort of rash, very common here in summer. I asked if they did not think they were too young to trouble themselves with religion yet. To which one of them replied, 'If it will be reasonable ten years hence to be religious, it is so now: I am not for deferring one moment.'

Thursday, 8 July – Mr Oglethorpe being there again, and casually speaking of sudden death, Miss Becky said, 'If it was the will of God, I should choose to die without a lingering illness.' Her sister said, 'Are you, then, prepared to die?' She replied, 'Jesus Christ is always prepared to help me. And little stress is to be laid on such a preparation for death as is made in a fit of sickness.'

Saturday, 10 July – Just as they had done drinking tea, Mrs Margaret, seeing [Miss Bovey's] colour change, asked if she was well. She did not return any answer; and Dr Tailfer soon after going by, she desired him to step in. He looked earnestly at her, felt her pulse, and replied, 'Well, madam, your sister is dying!' However, he thought it not impossible bleeding might help. She bled about an ounce, leaned back, and died.

I never saw so beautiful a corpse in my life. Poor comfort to its late inhabitant!

This evening we had such a storm of thunder and lightning as I never saw before, even in Georgia. This voice of God, too, told me I was not fit to die; since I was afraid rather than desirous of it. Oh, when shall I wish to be dissolved and to be with Christ? When I love him with all my heart.

Almost the whole town was the next evening at the funeral; where many, doubtless, made a world of good resolutions. Oh, how little trace of most of these will be left in the morning!

Tuesday, 20 July – Five of the Chicasaw Indians came to see us, with Mr Andrews, their interpreter. They were all warriors, four of them head men. The two chief were Paustoobee and Mingo Mattaw. Our conference was as follows:

Q. Do you believe there is one above who is over all things?

Paustoobee answered, We believe there are four beloved things above: the clouds, the sun, the clear sky, and he that lives in the clear sky.

Q. Do you think he made the sun, and the other beloved things?

A. We cannot tell. Who hath seen?

Q. Do you think he made you?

A. We think he made all men at first.

Q. How did he make them at first?

A. Out of the ground.

Q. Do you believe he loves you?

A. I do not know. I cannot see him.

Q. But has he not often saved your life?

A. He has. Many bullets have gone on this side and many on that side; but he would never let them hurt me.

Q. Then, cannot he save you from your enemies now?

A. Yes, but we know not if he will. We have now so many enemies round about us, that I think of nothing but death. And if I am to die, I shall die, and I will die like a man. But if he will have me to live, I shall live.

Q. We have a book that tells us many things of the beloved ones above; would you be glad to know them?

A. We have no time now but to fight. If we should ever be at peace, we should be glad to know.

Tuesday, 10 August – I set out for Frederica. In walking to Thunderbolt I was in so heavy a shower, that all my clothes were as wet as if I had gone through the river. I cannot but observe that vulgar error concerning the hurtfulness of the rains and dews of America. I have been thoroughly wet with these rains more than once, yet without any harm at all. And I have lain many nights in the open air, and received all the dews that fell; and so, I believe, might any one, if his constitution was not impaired by the softness of a genteel education.

Tuesday, 12 October – We considered if anything could yet be done for the poor people of Frederica; and I submitted to the judgement of my friends, which was that I should take another journey thither.

Monday, 18 October – Finding there were several Germans at Frederica who, not understanding the English tongue, could not join in our public servce, I desired them to meet me at my house, which they did every day at noon from thenceforward. We first sang a German hymn, then I read a chapter in the New Testament; then explained it to them as well as my little skill in the tongue would allow.

Tuesday, 23 October – Mr Oglethorpe sailed for England, leaving Mr Ingham, Mr Delamotte, and me at Savannah, but with less prospect of preaching to the Indians than we had the first day we set foot in America. Whenever I mentioned it, it was immediately replied, 'You cannot leave Savannah without a minister.' To this indeed my plain answer was, 'I openly declared both before, at, and ever since my coming hither that I neither would nor could take charge of the English any longer than till I could go among the Indians.' But though I had no other obligation not to leave Savannah now, yet I could not resist the importunate request of the more serious parishioners 'to watch over their souls yet a little longer till some one came who might supply my place.' And the time was not come to preach the gospel of peace to the heathen; all their nations being in a ferment; and Paustoobee and Mingo Mattaw having told me, 'Now our enemies are all about us, and we can do nothing but fight; but if the beloved ones should ever give us to be at peace, then we would hear the great Word.'

Wednesday, 22 December – Mr Delamotte and I, with a guide, set out to walk to the Cowpen.

1737

Saturday, 1 January – Our provisions fell short, our journey being longer than we expected; but having a little barbecued bear's flesh (that is, dried in the sun) we boiled it, and found it very wholesome food.

Sunday, 2 January – We came to the settlement of the Scotch Highlanders at Darien. I was surprised to hear an extempore prayer before a written sermon. Are not then the words we speak to God to be set in order at least as carefully as those we speak to our fellow worms?

Mr McLeod, their minister, is a serious, prudent, resolute, and (I hope) a pious man.

Wednesday, 5 January – We came to Frederica. Most of those we met with were, as we expected, cold and heartless. I could not find one who had retained his first love.

Wednesday, 26 January – After having beaten the air in this unhappy place for twenty days, at noon I took my final leave of Frederica. It was not any apprehension of my own danger, but an utter despair of doing good there, which made me content with the thought of seeing it no more.

Sunday, 3 April – [Savannah] This and every day in this great and holy week we had a sermon and the Holy Communion.

Monday, 4 April – I began learning Spanish, in order to converse with my Jewish parishioners; some of whom seem nearer the mind that was in Christ than many of those who call him Lord.

Tuesday, 12 April – Being determined, if possible, to put a stop to the proceedings of one in Carolina, who had married several of my parishioners without either banns or licence, I set out in a sloop for Charlestown. I related the case to Mr Garden, the Bishop of London's Commissary, who assured me he would take care no such irregularity should be committed for the future.

Friday, 22 April – It being the time of their annual Visitation, I had the pleasure of meeting the clergy of South Carolina. In the afternoon was such a conversation for several hours, on Christ our Righteousness, as I never heard in England in all the visitations I have been present at.

Wednesday, 18 May – I discovered the first convert to Deism that, I believe, has been made here. He was one that for some time had been zealously religious. But indulging himself in harmless company, he first made shipwreck of zeal, and then of his faith.

Wednesday, 25 May – I was sent for by one who desired to return to the Church of England; being deeply convinced by what I had occasionally preached, of the grievous errors the Church of Rome is in, and the great danger of continuing a member of it.

I cannot but observe the surprising infatuation that reigns in England. Advice upon advice did we receive there, to beware of the increase of Popery; but not one word do I remember to have heard of the increase of Infidelity.

Saturday, 25 June – Mr Causton, the store-keeper and chief magistrate was seized with a slow fever. I attended him every day and had a good hope from the thankfulness he showed that it would be a blessing.

Sunday, 3 July – Immediately after the Holy Communion, I mentioned to Mrs Williamson (Mr Causton's neice) something which I thought reprovable in her behaviour. She appeared extremely angry, and after a few minutes she turned about and went abruptly away.

Sunday, 7 August – I repelled Mrs Williamson from the Holy Communion.

Monday, 8 August – Mr Recorder issued the warrant following:

GEORGIA, SAVANNAH

To all Constables, Tithingmen, and others, whom these may concern:

YOU, and each of you, are hereby required to take the body of John Wesley, Clerk:
 And bring him before one of the bailiffs of the said town, to answer the complaint of William Williamson and Sophia his wife, for defaming the said Sophia, and refusing to administer to her the Sacrament of the Lord's Supper, in a public congregation, without cause. Given under my hand and seal the 8th day of August, *Anno Dom.* 1737 Theo Christie

Tuesday, 9 August – I was carried before the magistrates. Mr Jones, the constable, served the warrant. Mr Parker told me, 'However, you must appear at the next Court, holden for Savannah.' Mr Williamson said, 'Gentlemen, I desire Mr Wesley may give bail for his appearance.' But Mr Parker replied, 'Sir, Mr Wesley's word is sufficient.'

Thurday, 11 August – Mr Causton came again to my house. He said, 'Give the reasons of your repelling her before the whole congregation.' I answered, 'Sir, if you insist upon it, I will.' I wrote as follows:

To Mrs Sophia Williamson.

At Mr Causton's request, I write once more. The rules whereby I proceed are these:

'So many as intend to be partakers of the Holy Communion, shall signify their names to the Curate, at least some time the day before.

'And if any of these ... have done any wrong to his neighbours, by word or deed, so that the congregation be thereby offended, the Curate ... shall advertise him, that in any wise he presume not to come to the Lord's Table until he hath openly declared himself to have truly repented.'

If you offer yourself at the Lord's Table on Sunday, I will advertise you wherein you have done wrong. And when you have openly declared yourself to have truly repented, I will administer to you the mysteries of God. John Wesley
11 August 1737

Friday, 12 August – The rest of the family were very industrious in convincing all they could speak to 'that Mr Wesley had done this merely out of revenge because Sophy would not have him.'

Monday, 15 August – This evening was the last time Mr Causton was at church, or any of his family; Mrs Causton declaring she would come there no more while I stayed at Savannah.

Monday, 22 August – When the Court was met, Mr Causton gave a long charge to the Grand Jury, not to suffer any person to infringe their liberty or usurp an illegal authority over them. Forty-four jurors were then sworn, a great majority of whom were well prepared for their work, either by previous application from Mr Causton or by avowed enmity to me or to the Church of England. One was a Frenchman, who did not understand English, one a Papist, one a professed infidel, three Baptists, sixteen or seventeen other Dissenters; and several who had personal quarrels against me; and had openly vowed revenge.

Mrs Williamson's affidavit was next read, of which I desired a copy. Mr Causton answered that I might have one from any of the newspapers.

Then the Court delivered to the Grand Jury the following paper, entitled:

A LIST OF GRIEVANCES

That the said Revd. person deviates from the principles and regulations of the Established Church,

1. By inverting the order and method of the Liturgy;

2. By changing or altering such passages as he thinks proper in the version of Psalms publicly authorized.

3. By introducing compositions of psalms and hymns not inspected or authorized.

4. By introducing novelties, such as dipping infants, etc, in the Sacrament of Baptism;

5. By restricting the benefit of the Lord's Supper to a small number of persons, and refusing it to all others who will not conform to a grievous set of penances etc ...

6. By venting sundry uncharitable expressions of all who differ from him etc ...

7. By searching into and meddling with the affairs of private families etc ...

Friday, 2 September – Was the third Court at which I appeared. On the next Court-day I appeared again, but could not be heard, 'Because Mr Williamson was gone out of town.'

Friday, 7 October – I consulted my friends whether God did not call me to return to England. The reason for which I left it had now no force, there being no possibility, as yet, of instructing the Indians; neither had I, as yet, found or heard of any Indians on the continent of America who had the least desire of being instructed. After deeply considering these things, they were unanimous that I ought to go; but not yet.

Sunday, 30 October – The first English prayers lasted from five till half an hour past six. The Italian, which I read to a few Vaudois, began at nine. The second service for the English, including the sermon and the Holy Communion, continued from half an hour past ten till about half an hour past twelve. The French service began at one. At two I catechized the children.

About three began the English service. After this was ended, I had the happiness of joining with as many as my largest room would hold, in reading, prayer, and singing praise. And about six the service of the Moravians, so called, began; at which I was glad to be present, not as a teacher but a learner.

Thursday, 3 November – I appeared again at the Court holden on that day.

Tuesday, 22 November – Mr Anderson told me I had been reprimanded in the last Court, for an enemy to and hinderer of the public peace.

I again consulted my friends, who agreed with me that the time we looked for was now come. The next morning I went to Mr Causton again and told him I designed to set out for England immediately. I posted up an advertisement in the Great Square to the same effect, and then quietly prepared myself for the journey.

Friday, 2 December – I proposed to set out for Port Royal, Carolina, about noon. But about ten the magistrates sent for me, and told me I must not go out of the province; for I had not answered the allegations laid against me.

In the afternoon the magistrates published an order, requiring all the officers and sentinels to prevent my going out of the province, and forbidding any person to assist me to do so. Being now only a prisoner at large, in a place where I knew by experience every day would give fresh opportunity to procure evidence of words I never said, and actions I never did, I saw clearly the hour was come for leaving this place; and as soon as evening prayers were over, about eight o'clock, the tide then serving, I shook off the dust of my feet, and left Georgia, after having preached the gospel there not as I ought, but as I was able, one year and nearly nine months.

During this time I had frequent opportunities of making many observations and inquiries concerning the real state of this province which has been so variously represented, the English settlements therein, and the Indians.

[Here follows an account of the geography of Georgia, and Wesley's impressions of the Indian tribes.]

Saturday, 3 December – We came to Purrysburg early in the morning. Here I endeavoured to procure a guide to Port Royal. But none being to be had, we set out, an hour before sunrise. In half an hour we lost the path. About eleven we came into a large swamp, where we wandered up and down near three hours. Towards sunset we sat down on the ground, faint and weary enough. Our worst want was that of water. I thrust a cane we had into the ground, and, drawing it out, found the end moist. Upon which two of our company fell to digging with their hands, and at about three feet depth found good water. We thanked God, drank, and were much refreshed. After we had commended ourselves to God, we lay down close together, and I at least slept till morning.

Sunday, 4 December – God renewed our strength. We steered by the sun, as near as we could; between one and two God brought us safe to Benjamins Arieu's house, an old man whom we had left the day before. One undertook to guide us to Port Royal, which he said was between forty and fifty miles off. About sunset we asked our guide if he knew where he was, who frankly answered, 'No.' However, by the next evening, after many difficulties and delays, we landed on Port Royal Island.

Thursday, 8 December – Mr Delamotte came, with whom on Friday 9th I set out for Charlestown by water.

Tuesday, 13 December – Early we came to Charlestown, where I expected trials of a quite different nature, contempt and hunger being easy to be borne: but who can bear respect and fullness of bread?

Friday, 16 December – I parted from the last of those friends who came with me into America, Mr Charles Delamotte, from whom I had been but a few days separate since October 14, 1735.

Sunday, 18 December – I was seized with a violent flux, yet I had strength enough given to preach once more to this careless people.

Thursday, 22 December – I took my leave of America, though, if it please God, not for ever.

Saturday, 24 December – We sailed over Charlestown bar, and about noon lost sight of land.

1738

Sunday, 1 January – All in the ship, except the captain and steersman, were present both at the morning and evening service, and appeared as deeply attentive as even the poor people of Frederica did, while the word of God was new to their ears.

Monday, 2 January – I went several times the following days, with a design to speak to the sailors, but I was quite averse from speaking; I could not see how to make an occasion.

On Monday the 9th, and the following days, I reflected much on that vain desire, which had pursued me for so many years, of being in solitude in order to be a Christian. I have now, thought I, solitude. But am I therefore the nearer being a Christian? Not if Jesus Christ be the model of Christianity.

Tuesday, 24 January – My mind was now full of thought, part of which I writ down as follows:

I went to America, to convert the Indians; but oh, who shall convert me? Who, what is he that will deliver me from this evil heart of unbelief? I have a fair summer religion. I can talk well; nay, and believe myself, while no danger is near. But let death look me in the face, and my spirit is troubled. Nor can I say, 'To me to die is gain'! Oh, who will deliver me from this fear of death? Where shall I fly from it? A wise man advised me some time since, 'Be still, and go on.' Perhaps this is best, when it comes, to let it humble me, and at other times, to take no thought about it, but quietly to go on 'in the work of the Lord.'

Sunday, 29 January – We saw English land once more, which about noon appeared to be the Lizard Point. We ran by it with a fair wind, and at noon the next day made the west end of the Isle of Wight.

Toward evening was a calm; but in the night a strong north wind brought us safe into the Downs. The day before, Mr Whitefield had sailed out, neither of us then knowing anything of the other. At four in the morning we took board and in half an hour landed at Deal.

It is now two years and almost four months since I left my native country, in order to teach the Georgian Indians the nature of Christianity. But what have I learned myself in the meantime? Why, what I the least of all suspected, that I, who went to America to convert others, was never myself converted to God.

If it be said that I have faith, I answer, so have the devils – a sort of faith; but the faith I want is 'a sure trust and confidence in God, that, through the merits of Christ, my sins are forgiven, and I reconciled to the favour of God.' I want that faith which none can have without knowing that he hath it (though many imagine they have it, who have it not); for whosoever hath it, is 'freed from sin,' and he is freed from doubt, 'having the love of God shed abroad in his heart, through the Holy Ghost which is given unto him'; which 'Spirit itself beareth witness with his spirit that he is a child of God.'

Wednesday, 1 February – I left Deal, and came in the evening to Faversham. I here read prayers, and explained the Second Lesson to a few of those who were called Christians, but were indeed more savage in their behaviour than the wildest Indians I have yet met with.

Friday, 3 February – I came to Mr Delamotte's at Blendon. In the evening I came once more to London. Many reasons I have to bless God, for my having been carried into that strange land. Hereby I trust he hath in some measure 'humbled me and proved me, and shown me what was in my heart'. Hereby I have been taught to 'beware of men.' Hereby I am delivered from the fear of the sea, which I had both dreaded and abhorred from my youth.

I hope, too, some good may come to others hereby. All in Georgia have heard the word of God. A few steps have been taken towards publishing the glad tidings both to the African and American heathen.

Saturday, 4 February – I told my friends some of the reasons which a little hastened my return to England.

Sunday, 5 February – [Westminster] In the afternoon I was desired to preach at St John the Evangelist's. I did so on those strong words, 'If any man be in Christ, he is a new creature.' I was afterwards informed, many of the best in the parish were so offended, that I was not to preach there any more.

Tuesday, 7 February – (A day to be remembered.) At the house of a Dutch merchant, I met Peter Böhler [and others] just then landed from Germany. I offered to procure them a lodging, and did so near Mr Hutton's, where I then was. And from this time I did not willingly lose any opprotunity of conversing with them.

Wednesday, 8 February – I waited on the Board of Trustees, and gave them a short but plain account of the state of the colony: an account, I fear, not a little differing from those which they had frequently received before.

Sunday, 12 February – I preached at St Andrew's, Holborn. Here, too, it seems, I am to preach no more.

Saturday, 18 February – All this time I conversed much with Peter Böhler; but I understood him not, and least of all when he said, 'My brother, my brother, that philosophy of yours must be purged away.'

Sunday, 26 February – I preached at six at St Lawrence's; at ten in St Katharine Cree's church; and in the afternoon at St John's, Wapping. I believe it pleased God to bless the first sermon most, because it gave most offence.

Monday, 27 February – I took coach for Salisbury, and had several opportunities of conversing seriously with my fellow travellers.

Thurday, 2 March – I now renewed and wrote down my former resolutions:

1. To use absolute openness and unreserve with all I should converse with.

2. To labour after continual seriousness, not willingly indulging myself in any the least levity of behaviour, or in laughter – no, not for a moment.

3. To speak no word which does not tend to the glory of God; in particular, not to talk of worldly things.

Saturday, 4 March – I found my brother at Oxford, recovering from his pleurisy; and with him Peter Böhler, by whom (in the hand of the great God) I was, on Sunday the 5th, clearly convinced of unbelief, of the want of that faith whereby alone we are saved.

Immediately it struck into my mind, 'Leave off preaching. How can you preach to others, who have not faith yourself?' I asked Böhler whether he thought I should leave it off or not. He answered, 'By no means.' I asked, 'But what can I preach?' He said, 'Preach faith *till* you have it; and then, *because* you have it, you *will* preach faith.'

Monday, 6 March – I began preaching this new doctrine, though my soul started back from the work. The first person to whom I offered salvation by faith alone was a prisoner under sentence of death. His name was Clifford. Peter Böhler had many times desired me to speak to him before. But I could not prevail on myself so to do; being still a zealous assertor of the impossibility of a death-bed repentance.

Thursday, 23 March – I met Peter Böhler again, who now amazed me more and more by the account he gave of the fruits of living faith – the holiness and happiness which he affirmed to attend it. The next morning I began the Greek Testament again, being confident that God would hereby show me whether this doctrine was of God.

Sunday, 26 March – I preached at Whitam on 'the new creature', and went in the evening to a society in Oxford, where after using a collect or two and the Lord's Prayer, I expounded a chapter in the New Testament, and concluded with three or four more collects and a psalm.

Monday, 27 March – Mr Kinchin went with me to the Castle, where, after reading prayers, and preaching, we prayed with the condemned man, first in several forms of prayer, and then in such words as were given us in that hour. He kneeled down in much heaviness and confusion. After a space he rose up, and eagerly said, 'I am now ready to die. I know Christ has taken away my sins; and there is no more condemnation for me.'

Saturday, 1 April – At Mr Fox's society, my heart was so full that I could not confine myself to the forms of prayer which we were accustomed to use; neither do I purpose to be confined to them any more; but to pray with a form or without, as I may find suitable to particular occasions.

Saturday, 22 April – I met Peter Böhler once more. I had now no objection to what he said of the nature of faith; but I could not understand how this faith should be given in a moment: how a man could *at once* be thus turned from darkness to light, from sin and misery to righteousness and joy in the Holy Ghost. I searched the Scriptures again, particularly the Acts of the Apostles: but, to my utter astonishment, found scarce any instances there of other than *instantaneous* conversions. I had but one retreat left; namely, '*Thus*, I grant, God wrought in the *first* ages of Christianity; but the times are changed.'

But on Sunday the 23rd, I was beat out of this retreat too. Several living witnesses testified God had thus wrought in themselves, giving them in a moment such a faith in the blood of his Son as translated them out of darkness into light. Here ended my disputing. I could now only cry out, 'Lord, help thou my unbelief!'

I asked Peter Böhler again whether I ought not to refrain from teaching others. He said, 'No; do not hide in the earth the talent God hath given you.' Accordingly, on Tuesday the 25th, I spoke

clearly at Blendon of the nature ⸺
was very angry, and told me I did no⸺
done by talking thus.

Wednesday, 26 April – At Gerrard's Cross I plain⸺
those whom God gave into my hands the faith as it is in⸺
did next day to a young man I overtook on the road, and⸺
evening to our friends at Oxford.

Monday, 1 May – The return of my brother's illness obliged me
again to hasten to London. In the evening I found him at James
Hutton's, better as to his health but strongly averse from what he
called 'the new faith.'

This evening our little society began, which afterwards met in
Fetter Lane. Our fundamental rules were as follow:

1. That we will meet together once a week to 'confess our faults
one to another, and pray one for another, that we may be healed.'

2. That the persons so meeting be divided into several *bands*, or
little companies, none of them consisting of fewer than five or
more than ten persons.

3. That every one in order speak as freely, plainly, and
concisely as he can, the real state of his heart, since the last time of
meeting.

4. That all the bands have a conference at eight every
Wednesday evening, begun and ended with singing and prayer.

5. That any who desire to be admitted into the society be asked,
'Will you be entirely open; using no kind of reserve?'...

9. That every fourth Saturday be observed as a day of general
intercession.

10. That on the Sunday seven-night following be a general
lovefeast, from seven till ten in the evening.

Wednesday, 3 May – My brother had a long conversation with
Peter Böhler. And it now pleased God to open his eyes; so that he
also saw clearly the nature of that one true living faith, whereby
alone, 'through grace, we are saved.'

Tuesday, 9 May – I preached at Great St Helen's, to a very
numerous congregation, on 'he that spared not his own Son, but

...d him up for us all, how shall he not with him also freely give us all things?' I did not wonder in the least when I was afterwards told, 'Sir, you must preach here no more.'

Wednesday, 10 May – Mr Stonehouse, vicar of Islington, was convinced of 'the truth as it is in Jesus'. From this time till Saturday the 13th, I was sorrowful and very heavy; being neither able to read, nor meditate, nor sing, nor pray. Yet I was a little refreshed by Peter Böhler's letter.

Sunday, 21 May (Whitsunday) – I preached at St John's Wapping, at three, and at St Benet's, Paul's Wharf, in the evening. At these churches likewise I am to preach no more.

Monday, Tuesday, and Wednesday, I had 'continual sorrow and heaviness' in my 'heart'. What occured on Wednesday the 24th, I think best to relate at large.

I think it was about five this morning, that I opened my Testament on those words, 'There are given unto us exceeding great and precious promises, even that ye should be partakers of the divine nature' (2 Peter 1:4). Just as I went out, I opened it again on 'Thou art not far from the kingdom of God.' In the afternoon I was asked to go to St Paul's. The anthem was, 'Out of the deep have I called unto thee, O Lord: Lord, hear my voice.'

In the evening I went very unwillingly to a society in Aldersgate Street, where one was reading Luther's preface to the *Epistle to the Romans*. About a quarter before nine, while he was describing the change which God works in the heart through faith in Christ, I felt my heart strangely warmed. I felt I did trust in Christ, Christ alone for salvation; and an assurance was given me that he had taken away *my* sins, even *mine*, and saved *me* from the law of sin and death.

I began to pray with all my might for those who had in a more especial manner despitefully used me and persecuted me. I then testified openly to all there what I now first felt in my heart. But it was not long before the enemy suggested, 'This cannot be faith; for where is thy joy?' Then was I taught that peace and victory over sin are essential to faith in the Captain of our salvation; but that, as to the transports of joy that usually attend the beginning of it, especially in those who have mourned deeply, God sometimes giveth, sometimes withholdeth them.

After my return home, I was much buffetted with temptations; but cried out, and they fled away. They returned again and again. I as often lifted up my eyes, and he 'sent me help from his holy place.' And herein I found the difference between this and my former state. I was striving, with all my might under the law, as well as under grace. But then I was sometimes, if not often, conquered; now, I was always conqueror.

Thursday, 25 May – The moment I awaked, 'Jesus, Master,' was in my heart and in my mouth; and I found all my strength lay in keeping my eye fixed upon him, and my soul waiting on him continually. Being again at St Paul's I could taste the good word of God in the anthem, which began, 'My song shall be always of the loving-kindness of the Lord.' Yet the enemy injected a fear, 'If thou dost believe, why is there not a more sensible change?' I answered (yet not I), 'That I know not. But this I know, I have now "peace with God".'

Friday, 26 May – My soul continued in peace, but yet in heaviness because of manifold temptations. I asked Mr Töltschig what to do. He said, 'You must not fight with them, but flee from them the moment they appear, and take shelter in the wounds of Jesus.'

Saturday, 27 May – Believing one reason of my want of joy was want of time for prayer, I resolved to do no business till I went to church in the morning, but to continue pouring out my heart before him.

Sunday, 28 May – I waked in peace, but not in joy. In the same even quiet state I was till the evening, when I was roughly attacked in a large company as an enthusiast, a seducer, and a setter-forth of new doctines. By the blessing of God, I was not moved to anger.

I preached in the morning at St George's Bloomsbury, on 'This is the victory that overcometh the world, even our faith.'

Sunday, 4 June – Was indeed a feast-day. For from the time of my rising till past one in the afternoon, I was praying, reading the

Scriptures, singing praise, or calling sinners to repentance. I saw more than ever that the gospel is in truth but one great promise, from the beginning of it to the end.

Tuesday, 6 June – I received a letter which threw me into much perplexity. After some hours spent in the Scripture and prayer, I was much comforted. Yet I felt a kind of soreness in my heart, so that I found my wound was not fully healed.

Wednesday, 7 June – I determined, if God should permit, to retire for a short time into Germany.

Wednesday, 14 June – About four in the afternoon we lost sight of England. We reached the Meuse on Thursday morning, and in an hour and a half landed at Rotterdam. We were eight in all: five English and three Germans. I never before saw any such road as this. For many miles together it is raised for some yards above the level, and paved with a small sort of brick, as smooth and clean as the Mall in St. James's. At Gouda, we were a little surprised at meeting with a treatment which is not heard of in England. Several inns utterly refused to entertain us; so that it was with difficulty we at last found one where they did us the favour to take our money for some meat and drink and the use of two or three bad beds.

Saturday, 17 June – [Ysselstein] In the morning some of our English brethren desired me to administer the Lord's Supper. The rest of the day we spent in hearing the wonderful work which God is beginning to work over all the earth; and in making our requests known unto him, and giving him thanks for the mightiness of his kingdom.

At six in the morning we took boat. The beautiful gardens lie on both sides of the river for the great part of the way to Amsterdam, whither we came about five in the evening. The exact neatness of all the buildings, the nice cleanness of the streets, and the canals which run through all the main streets with trees on either side, make this the pleasantest city which I have ever seen. Here we were entertained, with truly Christian hospitality.

Monday, 27 June – [In Germany] Having a few hours' walk to Cologne we went thither easily, and came at five the next evening into the ugliest city I ever yet saw with my eyes.

Wednesday, 28 June – We went to the cathedral, which is mere heaps upon heaps; a huge, mis-shapen thing, which has no more of symmetry than of neatness belonging to it.

At four we took boat, when I could not but observe the decency of the Papists. As soon as ever we were seated they all pulled off their hats, and each used by himself a short prayer for our prosperous journey. I never heard one of them take the name of God in vain, or saw any one laugh when anything of religion was mentioned.

Monday, 3 July – [Frankfurt] Faint and weary as we were, we could have no admittance here, having brought no passes with us; which indeed we never imagined would have been required in a time of settled general peace. After waiting an hour at the gates we procured a messenger, whom we sent to Peter Böhler's father; who immediately procured us entrance into the city, and entertained us in the most friendly manner. I was so ill that, after talking a little with Count Zinzendorf, I was forced to lie down the rest of the day.

Tuesday, 4 July – The family at Marienborn consists of about ninety persons, gathered out of many nations. They live in a large house hired by the Count. 'Oh, how pleasant a thing it is for brethren to dwell together in unity!'

Friday, 7 July – I usually spent the day, chiefly in conversation with those who could speak either Latin or English. And here I continually met with living proofs of the power of faith: persons saved from inward as well as outward sin by 'the love of God shed abroad in their hearts.'

Monday, 24 July – At Jenna the stone pillars begin, set up by the Elector of Saxony, and marking out every quarter of a German mile. Every mile is a large pillar, with the names of the neighbouring towns, and their distances inscribed. It were much to be wished that the same care were taken in England.

Sunday, 30 July – [Meissen] After breakfast we went to church. I was greatly surprised at the costliness of apparel in many, and the gaudiness of it in more; at the huge fur caps worn by the women, which generally had one or more ribands hanging down a great length behind. The minister's habit was adorned with gold and scarlet, and a vast cross both behind and before. Most of the congregation sat (the men generally with their hats on), and all of them stayed during the Holy Communion though but very few received. Alas, alas! what a *Reformed* country is this!

At two in the afternoon we came to Dresden. The new church on the outside resembles a theatre. It is eight-square, built of fine freestone. We were desired also to take notice of the great bridge; of the large brass crucifix upon it, and of the late King Augustus's statue on horseback. Alas! where will all these things appear when the earth and the works thereof shall be burned up?

Tuesday, 1 August – At three in the afternoon I came to Herrnhut, about thirty English miles from Dresden. It lies on the border of Bohemia, and contains about a hundred houses, built on a rising ground, with evergreen woods on two sides, gardens and cornfields on the others, and high hills at a small distance. It has one long street. Fronting the middle is the Orphan House; in the lower part of which is the apothecary's shop, in the upper the chapel, capable of containing six or seven hundred people. At the east end of it is the Count's house – a small, plain building like the rest.

We had a convenient lodging assigned us in the house appointed for strangers. About eight we went to the public service, at which they frequently use other instruments with their organ. They began with singing. Then followed the expounding, closed by a second hymn. Prayer followed; then a few verses of a third hymn, which concluded the service.

Thursday, 3 August – Every day at eleven, I was at the Bible Conference, wherein Mr Müller and others read a portion of Scriptures in the original. At five was the conference for strangers, when several questions concerning justification were resolved.

On Friday and Saturday (and every day in the following week) I had conversation with the most experienced brethren concerning the great work which God had wrought in their souls; and with the teachers and elders of the Church, concerning the discipline used therein.

Tuesday, 8 August – A child was buried. Seeing the father (a tailor by trade) looking at the grave, I asked, 'How do you find yourself?' He said, 'Praise be the Lord, never better. He has taken the soul of my child to himself. I have seen, according to my desire, his body committed to holy ground. And I know that when it is raised again, both he and I shall be ever with the Lord.'

Four times I enjoyed the blessing of hearing [Christian David] preach during the few days I spent here; every time he chose the very subject which I should have desired. Thrice he described the state of those who are 'weak in faith', who are justified, but have not yet a new, clean heart; who have received forgiveness through the blood of Christ, but have not received the constant in-dwelling of the Holy Ghost.

Saturday the 12th was the Intercession-day, when many strangers were present, some of whom came twenty or thirty miles. I would gladly have spent my life here; but my Master calling me to labour in another part of his vineyard, on Monday the 14th I was constrained to take my leave of this happy place.

[Here follow some Moravian 'testimonies', and Wesley's account of the discipline of 'the Church of Herrnhut' including:]

AN EXTRACT OF THE CONSTITUTION OF
THE CHURCH OF THE MORAVIAN BRETHREN AT HERRNHUT

Towards magistrates, we bear the greatest reverence. We cheerfully submit to their laws; and even when many of us have been spoiled of their goods, driven out of their houses, and every way oppressed by them, yet they resisted them not, neither opening their mouths nor lifting up their hands against them.

We have also Censors and Monitors. The Censors signify what they observe either to the Deacons or Monitors. Some Monitors there are whom all know to be such; others who are secretly appointed; and who, if need require, may freely admonish, in the love of Christ, even the rulers of the Church.

In the year 1727 four-and-twenty men, and as many women, agreed that each of them would spend an hour in every day in praying to God for his blessing on his people. They pour out their souls before God, not only for their own brethren, but also for other churches and persons that have desired to be mentioned in their prayers. And this perpetual intercession has never ceased day or night, since its first beginning.

Our little children we instruct chiefly by hymns; whereby we find the most important truths most successfully insinuated into their minds.

We highly reverence marriage, as greatly conducive to the kingdom of Christ. But neither our young men nor women enter into it till they assuredly know they are married to Christ.

They have a peculiar esteem for lots; and, accordingly use them both in public and private, to decide points of importance, when the reasons brought on each side appear to be of equal weight. And they believe this to be then the only way of wholly setting aside their own will, and clearly knowing what is the will of God.

Two men keep watch every night in the street; as do two women, in the women's apartment; that they may pour out their souls for those that sleep, and by their hymns raise the hearts of any who are awake to God.

Saturday, 2 September – We came to Cologne, and between seven and eight reached a village, an hour short of Neus. Here we overtook a large number of Switzers – men, women and children, singing, dancing, and making merry, being all going *to make their fortunes in Georgia*. Looking upon them as delivered into my hands by God, I plainly told them what manner of place it was. If they now leap into the fire with open eyes, their blood is on their own head!

Sunday, 17 September – I began again to declare in my own country the glad tidings of salvation, preaching three times, and afterwards expounding the Holy Scripture to a large company in the Minories. On Monday I rejoiced to meet with our little society, which now consisted of thirty-two persons. The next day I went to the condemned felons in Newgate, and offered them free salvation. The next evening I spoke the truth in love at a society in Aldersgate Street. Some contradicted at first, but not long.

Sunday, 1 October – I preached both morning and afternoon at St George's-in-the-East. On the following days I endeavoured to explain the way of salvation to many who had misunderstood what had been preached concerning it.

Friday, 6 October – I went to the Rev. Mr Bedford, to tell him, between me and him alone, of the injury he had done both to God and his brother by preaching and printing that very weak sermon on assurance. The assurance we preach is of quite another kind from what he writes against.

In the evening I began expounding at a little society in Wapping. On Sunday the 8th I preached at the Savoy Chapel on the Pharisee and Publican.

Monday, 9 October – I set out for Oxford. In walking I read the truly surprising narrative of the conversions lately wrought in and about the town of Northampton, in New England. Surely 'this is the Lord's doing, and it is marvellous in our eyes.'

Sunday, 5 November – I preached at St Botolph's, Bishopsgate; in the afternoon, at Islington; and in the evening, to such a congregation as I never saw before, at St Clement's in the Strand. As this was the first time of my preaching here, I suppose it is to be the last.

On Wednesday my brother and I went, to do the last good office to the condemned malefactors. It was the most glorious instance I ever saw of faith triumphing over sin and death. One observing the tears run fast down the cheeks of one in particular, while his eyes were steadily fixed upwards, a few moments before he died, asked, 'How do you feel your heart now?' He calmly replied, 'I feel a peace which I could not have believed to be possible. And I know it is the peace of God, which passeth all understanding.'

My brother took that occasion of declaring the gospel of peace to a large assembly of publicans and sinners.

Saturday, 11 November – I spent the evening with a little company at Oxford. I was grieved to find prudence had made them leave off singing psalms. I fear it will not stop here. God deliver me, from whatever the world calls Christian prudence!

Sunday, 12 November – In the following week I began to inquire what the doctrine of the Church of England is concerning justification by faith; and the sum of what I found in the Homilies I extracted and printed for the use of others.

Monday, 20 November – I was greatly troubled in dreams; and about eleven o'clock waked in an unaccountable consternation. About that time (as I found in the morning) one who had been designed to be my pupil, came into the Porter's lodge with a pistol in his hand. He presented this, as in sport, first at one and then at another. He then attempted twice or thrice to shoot himself, but it would not go off. Upon his laying it down one took it up, and blew out the priming. He was very angry, went and got fresh prime, sat down, and about twelve, pulling off his hat and wig, said he would die like a gentleman, and shot himself through the head.

Sunday, 3 December – I began reading prayers at Bocardo (the city prison), which had been long discontinued. In the afternoon I received a letter earnestly desiring me to publish my account of Georgia; and another as earnestly dissuading me from it, 'because it would bring much trouble upon me'.

Monday, 11 December – Hearing Mr Whitefield was arrived from Georgia, I hastened to London; and on Tuesday the 12th God gave us to take sweet counsel together.

Sunday, 17 December – I preached in the afternoon at Islington. In the evening at St Swithin's for the last time. Sunday the 24th I preached at Great St Bartholomew's in the morning and at Islington in the afternoon; where we had the blessed sacrament every day this week, and were comforted on every side.

1739

'Had the pleasure of introducing my honoured and revered friend, Mr John Wesley, to preach at Blackheath. The Lord give him ten thousand times more success than he has given me!'

George Whitefield, *Journal*, 14 June 1739

'Dear, honoured sir, if you have any regard for the peace of the church, keep in your sermon on predestination. But you have cast a lot!... The Lord direct us all!'

George Whitefield, letter to John Wesley, 2 July 1739

Monday, 1 January – Mr Hall, Kinchin, Ingham, Whitefield, Hutchins, and my brother Charles were present at our lovefeast in Fetter Lane, with about sixty of our brethren. About three in the morning, as we were continuing instant in prayer, the power of God came mightily upon us, insomuch that many cried out for exceeding joy, and many fell to the ground. As soon as we were recovered a little from that awe and amazement at the presence of his majesty we broke out with one voice, 'We praise thee, O God; we acknowledge thee to be the Lord.'

Sunday, 21 January – We were greatly surprised in the evening, while I was expounding in the Minories. A well-dressed, middle-aged woman suddenly cried out as in the agonies of death. She continued so to do for some time. When she was a little recovered, I desired her to call upon me the next day. She told me that about three years before she was under strong convictions of sin, and in such terror of mind that she had no comfort in anything, nor any rest day or night: that she sent for the minister of her parish, and told him the distress she was in: upon which he told her husband she was stark mad, and advised him to send for a physician immediately. A physician was sent for accordingly, who ordered her to be blooded, blistered, and so on. But this did not heal her wounded spirit. So that she continued much as she was before: till the last night, he whose word she at first found to be 'sharper than any two-edged sword' gave her a faint hope that he would undertake her cause, and heal the soul which had sinned against him.

Thursday, 15 March – I had no thought of leaving London, when I received a letter from Mr Whitefield, and another from Mr Seward, entreating me in the most pressing manner to come to Bristol without delay. This I was not at all forward to do.

Wednesday, 28 March – My journey was proposed to our society in Fetter Lane. But my brother Charles would scarce bear the mention of it; till, appealing to the oracles of God, he received those words as spoken to himself, 'Son of man, behold, I take from thee the desire of thine eyes with a stroke: yet shalt thou not mourn or weep.' Our other brethren, however, continuing the dispute, we at length all agreed to decide it by lot. And by this it was determined I should go.

Saturday, 31 March – In the evening I reached Bristol, and met Mr Whitefield. I could scarce reconcile myself at first to this strange way of preaching in the fields, of which he set me an example on Sunday; having been all my life (till very lately) so tenacious of every point relating to decency and order, that I should have thought the saving of souls almost a sin if it had not been done in a church.

Sunday, 1 April – In the evening, I begun expounding our Lord's Sermon on the Mount (one pretty remarkable precedent of field-preaching) to a little society in Nicholas Street.

Monday, 2 April – At four in the afternoon I submitted to be more vile, and proclaimed in the highways the glad tidings of salvation, speaking from a little eminence in a ground adjoining to the city, to about three thousand people. The scripture on which I spoke was 'The Spirit of the Lord is upon me, because he hath anointed me to preach the gospel to the poor.'

Wednesday, 4 April – In the evening three women agreed to meet together weekly, with the same intention as those at London – 'to confess their faults one to another, and pray one for another, that they may be healed.' At eight four young men agreed to meet, in pursuance of the same design.

Sunday, 8 April – At seven in the morning I preached to about a thousand persons at Bristol, and afterwards to about fifteen hundred on the top of Hanham Mount in Kingswood. About five thousand were in the afternoon at Rose Green; among whom I stood and cried, in the name of the Lord, 'If any man thirst, let him come unto me and drink.'

Saturday, 14 April – I preached at the Poor-house; three or four hundred were within, and more than twice that number without: to whom I explained those comfortable words, 'When they had nothing to pay, he frankly forgave them both.'

Sunday, 15 April – I explained at seven to five or six thousand persons the story of the Pharisee and the Publican. About three thousand were present at Hanham Mount. I preached at Newgate after dinner. Between five and six we went to Rose Green: it rained hard at Bristol, but not a drop fell upon us, while I declared to about five thousand, 'Christ, our wisdom, and righteousness, and sanctification, and redemption.'

Tuesday, 17 April – The room in which we were was propped beneath, but the weight of people made the floor give way; the post which propped it fell down with a great noise. But the floor sank no further; so that, after a little surprise at first, they quietly attended to the things that were spoken.

Saturday, 21 April – At Weavers' Hall a young man was suddenly seized with a violent trembling all over, and in a few minutes, sunk down to the ground. But we ceased not calling upon God, till he raised him up full of 'peace and joy in the Holy Ghost.'

Tuesday, 24 April – I preached at four in the afternoon to the poor colliers, at a place about the middle of Kingswood, called Two-Mile-Hill.

Sunday, 29 April – I declared the free grace of God to about four thousand people from those words, 'He that spared not his own Son, but delivered him up for us all, how shall he not with him also freely give us all things?' I then went to Clifton, at the minister's desire, who was dangerously ill, and thence returned to a little plain, near Hanham Mount, where about three thousand were present. After dinner I went to Clifton again. The church was quite full at the prayers and sermon, as was the churchyard at the burial which followed. From Clifton we went to Rose Green, where were, by computation, near seven thousand, and thence to Gloucester Lane society. After which was our first lovefeast in Baldwin Street. Oh how has God renewed my strength! who used ten years ago to be so faint and weary with preaching *twice* in one day!

Tuesday, 1 May – At Baldwin Street my voice could scarce be heard amidst the groanings of some and cries of others, calling aloud to him that is 'mighty to save'.

Tuesday, 8 May – I went to Bath, but was not suffered to be in the meadow where I was before; which occasioned the offer of a much more convenient place, where I preached Christ to about a thousand souls.

Wednesday, 9 May – We took possession of a piece of ground in the Horsefair, where it was designed to build a room, large enough to contain both the societies of Nicholas and Baldwin Streets, and such of their acquaintance as might desire to be present, at such times as the Scripture was expounded. And on Saturday the 12th the first stone was laid, with the voice of praise and thanksgiving.

Every morning now I read prayers and preached at Newgate. Every evening I expounded a portion of Scripture at one or more of the societies. On Monday, I preached abroad, near Bristol; on Tuesday, at Bath and Two-Mile-Hill alternately; on Wednesday, at Baptist Mills; every other Thursday, near Pensford; every other Friday, in another part of Kingswood; on Saturday afternoon, and Sunday morning, in the Bowling Green; on Sunday, at eleven near Hanham Mount, at two at Clifton, and at five on Rose Green; and hitherto, as my days, so my strength hath been.

Sunday, 20 May – Seeing many of the rich at Clifton Church, my heart was much pained for them, and I was earnestly desirous that some even of them might 'enter into the kingdom of heaven'.

Tuesday, 5 June – There was great expectation at Bath of what a noted man was to do to me there; and I was much entreated not to preach because no one knew what might happen. By this report I also gained a much larger audience, among whom were many of the rich and the great. I told them plainly the Scripture had concluded them all under sin – high and low, rich and poor, one with another. Many of them seemed to be a little surprised, and were sinking apace into seriousness, when their champion appeared, and, coming close to me, asked by what authority I did these things. I replied, 'By the authority of Jesus Christ, conveyed to me by the (now) Archbishop of Canterbury, when he laid hands upon me, and said, "Take thou authority to preach the gospel."' He said, 'This is a contrary to Act of Parliament: this is a conventicle.' I answered, 'Sir, the conventicles mentioned in that Act are seditious meetings; but here is no shadow of sedition; therefore it is not contrary to that Act.' He replied, 'I say it is; and, beside, your preaching frightens people out of their wits.' 'Sir, did you ever hear me preach?' 'No.' 'How, then, can you judge of what you never heard?' 'Sir, by common report.' 'Common report is not enough. Give me leave, sir, to ask, is not your name Nash?' 'My name is Nash.' 'Sir, I dare not judge of you by common report: I think it not enough to judge by.' Here he paused awhile, and, having recovered himself, said, 'I desire to know what this people comes here for': on which one replied, 'Sir, leave him to me; let an old woman answer him. You, Mr

Nash, take care of your body; we take care of our souls: and for the food of our souls we come here.' He replied not a word, but walked away.

Monday, 11 June – I received a pressing letter from London to come thither as soon as possible, our brethren in Fetter Lane being in great confusion for want of my presence and advice. After sermon I commended them to the grace of God, in whom they had believed. Surely God hath yet a work to do in this place.

Thursday, 14 June – I went with Mr Whitefield to Blackheath, where were, I believe, twelve or fourteen thousand people. He a little surprised me by desiring me to preach in his stead, which I did (though nature recoiled), on my favourite subject, 'Jesus Christ, who of God is made unto us wisdom, righteousness, sanctification, and redemption.'

I was greatly moved with compassion for the rich that were there. Some of them seemed to attend, while others drove away their coaches from so uncouth a preacher.

Saturday, 16 June – We met at Fetter Lane, to humble ourselves before God, and own he had justly withdrawn his Spirit from us for our manifold unfaithfulness: by our divisions; by our leaning again to our own works, and trusting in them, instead of Christ; and, above all, by blaspheming his work among us, imputing it either to nature, to the force of imagination, or even to the delusion of the devil. In that hour we found God with us as at the first.

Sunday, 17 June – I preached, at seven, in Upper Moorfields, to (I believe) six or seven thousand people, on, 'Ho! everyone that thirsteth, come ye to the waters.'

At five I preached on Kennington Common to about fifteen thousand people on, 'Look unto me, and be ye saved, all ye ends of the earth.'

Monday, 18 June – I left London early and the next evening reached Bristol, and preached to a numerous congregation.

Howell Harris called upon me an hour or two after. He said he had been much dissuaded from hearing or seeing me by many who said all manner of evil of me. 'But,' he said, 'as soon as I heard you preach I quickly found what spirit you was of. I was so overpowered with joy and love that I had much ado to walk home.'

It is scarce credible what advantage Satan had gained during my absence of only eight days. Disputes had crept into our little society, so that the love of many was already waxed cold. When we met in the evening, instead of reviving the dispute, we all betook ourselves to prayer. Our Lord was with us. Our divisions were healed, misunderstandings vanished away; and all our hearts were sweetly drawn together and united as at the first.

Friday, 22 June – In the afternoon I preached at the Fishponds, but had no life or spirit in me, and was much in doubt whether God would not lay me aside and send other labourers into his harvest.

Tuesday, 26 June – I preached near the house we had a few days before begun to build for a school, in the middle of Kingswood, under a little sycamore-tree, during a violent storm of rain, on those words, 'as the rain cometh down from heaven, and returneth not thither, but watereth the earth and maketh it bring forth and bud... so shall my word be: it shall not return unto me void; but it shall accomplish that which I please.'

Sunday, 1 July – I preached on the favourite advice of the infidel in Ecclesiastes (so zealously enforced by his brethren now), 'Be not righteous overmuch.'

A young woman sunk down at Rose Green in a violent agony both of body and mind; as did five or six persons in the evening at the new Room, at whose cries many were greatly offended.

I went to Mrs Thornhill's, whose nearest relations were earnestly dissuading her from being 'righteous overmuch'. She answered all they advanced with meekness and love, and continued steadfast and immovable. Endure hardship still, thou good soldier of Christ!

Friday, 6 July – In the afternoon I was with Mr Whitefield, just come from London; he preached concerning 'the Holy Ghost, which all who believe are to receive'; not without a just, though severe, censure of those who preach as if there were no Holy Ghost.

Saturday, 7 July – I had an opportunity to talk with him of those outward signs which had so often accompanied the inward work of God. I found his objections were chiefly grounded on gross misrepresentations of matters of fact. But the next day he had an opportunity of informing himself better: for no sooner had he begun in his sermon to invite all sinners to believe in Christ, than four persons sunk down close to him. One lay without sense or motion; a second trembled exceedingly; the third had strong convulsions but made no noise, unless by groans; the fourth, equally convulsed, called upon God, with strong cries and tears. From this time, I trust, we shall all suffer God to carry on his own work in the way that pleaseth him.

Tuesday, 17 July – I rode to Bradford, five miles from Bath, whither I had been long invited to come. I went to a gentleman in the town who had been present at Bath, and, with the strongest marks of sincerity and affection, wished me good luck in the name of the Lord. But it was past. I found him now quite cold. He began disputing; and at last told me plainly one of our own college had informed him they always took me to be a little crack-brained at Oxford.

Sunday, 22 July – As I was explaining 'Blessed are the poor in spirit' to about three thousand people, we had a fair opportunity of showing all men what manner of spirit we were of; for in the middle of the sermon the press-gang came, and seized on one of the hearers (ye learned in the law, what becomes of Magna Charta, and of English liberty and property?); all the rest standing still, and none opening his mouth or lifting up his hand to resist them.

Friday, 17 August – Many of our society met, at one in the afternoon; and agreed that all the members should obey the Church to which we belong by observing all Fridays in the year as days of fasting or abstinence, and that as many as had opportunity should then meet, to spend an hour together in prayer.

Wednesday, 22 August – I was with many that were in heaviness: two of whom were soon filled with peace and joy. In the afternoon I endeavoured to guard the weak against what too often occasions heaviness – levity of temper of behaviour – from 'I said of laughter, it is mad; and of mirth, what doeth it?'

Monday, 3 September – I talked largely with my mother, who told me that, till a short time since, she had scarce heard such a thing mentioned as the having forgiveness of sins now, or God's Spirit bearing witness with our spirit; much less did she imagine that this was the common privilege of all true believers. 'But,' said she, 'two or three weeks ago, while my son Hall was pronouncing those words, in delivering the cup to me, "The blood of our Lord Jesus Christ, which was given for thee," the words struck through my heart, and I knew God for Christ's sake had forgiven *me* all *my* sins.'

Wednesday, 12 September – In the evening, at Fetter Lane, I described the life of faith. At eight I exhorted our brethren to keep close to the Church and to all the ordinances of God.

Thursday, 13 September – A serious clergyman desired to know in what points we differed from the Church of England. I answered, 'To the best of my knowledge, in none. The doctrines we preach are the fundamental doctrines of the Church, clearly laid down, in her Prayers, Articles, and Homilies.'

Thursday, 27 September – I went at six to Turner's Hall; which holds (by computation) two thousand persons. The press both within and without was very great. In the beginning of the expounding, there being a large vault beneath, the main beam which supported the floor broke. The floor immediately sunk, which occasioned much noise and confusion. But, two or three days before, a man had filled the vault with hogsheads of tobacco, so that the floor, after sinking a foot or two, rested upon them, and I went on without interruption.

Monday, 15 October – Upon a pressing invitation, some time since received, I set out for Wales. About four in the afternoon I preached on a little green, at the foot of The Ddefauden, to three or four hundred plain people.

Tuesday, 16 October – [Abergavenny] About a thousand people stood patiently (though the frost was sharp, it being after sunset) while, from Acts 28:22, I simply described the plain old religion of the Church of England, which is now almost everywhere spoken against, under the new name of Methodism. An hour after, I explained it a little more fully in a neighbouring house, showing how 'God hath exalted Jesus to be a Prince and a Saviour, to give repentance and remission of sins.'

Friday, 19 October – I preached in the morning at Newport to the most insensible, ill-behaved people I have ever seen in Wales. One ancient man, during a great part of the sermon, cursed and swore almost incessantly; and, towards the conclusion, took up a great stone, which he many times attempted to throw. But that he could not do. Such the champions, such the arms, against field-preaching!

Tuesday, 23 October – In riding to Bradford, I read over Mr Law's book on the New Birth: philosophical, speculative, precarious. At eleven I preached at Bearfield to about three thousand on the spirit of nature, of bondage and of adoption.

Thursday, 4 November – [Reading] A little company of us met in the evening; at which the zealous mob was so enraged, they were ready to tear the house down. Therefore I hope God has a work to do in this place. In thy time let it be fulfilled!

Tuesday, 13 November – A young gentleman overtook me on the road, and, after a while, asked me if I had seen Whitefield's Journals. I told him I had. 'And what do you think of them?' said he. 'Don't you think they are d–d cant, enthusiasm from end to end? I think so.' I asked him, 'Why do you think so?' He replied, 'Why, he talks so much about joy and stuff, and inward feelings. As I hope to be saved, I cannot tell what to make of it.' I asked,

'Did you ever feel the love of God in your heart? If not, how should you tell what to make of it? Whatever is spoke of the religion of the heart, and of the inward workings of the Spirit of God, must appear enthusiasm to those who have not felt them.'

Tuesday, 27 November – I writ a short account of what had been done in Kingswood, and of our present undertaking there, as follows:

Few persons have lived long in the West of England who have not heard of the colliers of Kingswood: a people famous, from the beginning, for neither fearing God nor regarding man; so ignorant of the things of God that they seemed but one remove from the beasts that perish; and therefore utterly without desire of instruction, as well as the means of it.

Many last winter used tauntingly to say of Mr Whitefield, 'If he will convert heathens, why does not he go to the colliers of Kingswood?' In the spring he did so. And as there were thousands who resorted to no place of worship, he went after them into their own wilderness, 'to seek and save that which was lost.' When he was called away, others went. And, by the grace of God, their labour was not in vain. The scene is already changed. Kingswood does not now, as a year ago, resound with cursing and blasphemy. It is no more filled with drunkenness and uncleanness, no longer full of wars and fightings, of wrath and envyings. Peace and love are there. Great numbers of the people are mild, gentle, and easy to be entreated. Hardly is their 'voice heard in the streets'; or, indeed, in their own wood, unless when they are at their usual evening diversion, singing praise unto God their Saviour.

Thursday, 13 December – [Oxford] During my short stay here I received several unpleasing accounts of the state of things in London.

Wednesday, 19 December – I accordingly came to London, though with a heavy heart. Here I found every day the dreadful effects of our brethren's reasoning and disputing with each other. Scarce one in ten retained his first love; and most of the rest were in the utmost confusion, biting and devouring one another.

Monday, 24 December – After spending part of the night at Fetter Lane, I went to a smaller company, where also we exhorted one another with hymns and spiritual songs, and poured out our hearts to God in prayer.

1740

'John Wesley being resolved to do all things himself... he will have the glory of doing all things.'

James Hutton, Moravian leader in the Fetter Lane Society, 1740

Tuesday, 1 January – I endeavoured to explain the true, Christian, scriptural stillness, by unfolding those solemn words, 'Be still, and know that I am God.'

Wednesday, 2 January – I earnestly besought them all to 'stand in the old paths,' and no longer to subvert one another's souls by idle controversies and strife of words.

Monday, 21 January – I preached at Hanham. In the evening I made a collection in our congregation for the relief of the poor, who having no work (because of the severe frost), and no assistance from the parish wherein they lived, were reduced to the last extremity. I made another collection on Thursday, and a third on Sunday; by which we were enabled to feed a hundred, sometimes a hundred and fifty a day, of those whom we found to need it most.

Monday, 3 March – I rode to Reading, where I had left two or three full of peace and love. But I now found some from London had been here, grievously troubling these souls also, labouring to persuade them (1) that they had no faith at all, because they sometimes felt doubt or fear; (2) that they ought to be still; not to go to church, not to communicate, not to search the Scriptures: 'because,' say they, 'you cannot do any of these things without trusting in them.'

Tuesday, 1 April – [Bristol] While I was expounding the twenty-third chapter of the Acts (how wonderfully suited to the occasion! though not by my choice) the floods began to lift up their voice. All the street was filled with people, shouting, cursing, and swearing, and ready to swallow the ground with fierceness and rage. The Mayor sent order that they should disperse. But they set him at nought. The chief constable came next in person, who was, till then, sufficiently prejudiced against us. But they insulted him also in so gross a manner as, I believe, fully opened his eyes. At length the Mayor sent several of his officers, who took the ringleaders into custody, and did not go till all the rest were dispersed.

Wednesday, 2 April – The rioters were brought up to the Quarter Sessions being held that day. They began to excuse themselves by saying many things of me. But the Mayor cut them all short, saying, 'What Mr Wesley is, is nothing to you. I will keep the peace: I will have no rioting in this city.'

Calling at Newgate in the afternoon, I was informed that the poor wretches under sentence of death were earnestly desirous to speak with me, but that it could not be, Alderman Beecher having just sent an express order that they should not. I cite Alderman Beecher to answer for these souls at the judgement-seat of Christ.

Wednesday, 23 April – [London, Fetter Lane] Mr Simpson told me all the confusion was owing to my brother, who would preach up the ordinances: 'whereas believers,' said he, 'are not subject to ordinances; and unbelievers have nothing to do with them. They ought to be still; otherwise they will be unbelievers all the days of their life.'

After a fruitless dispute of about two hours, I returned home with a heavy heart. In the evening our society met; but cold, weary, heartless, dead. I found nothing of brotherly love among them; but a harsh, dry, heavy, stupid spirit.

Tuesday, 24 June – [London] The substance of my exposition in the morning, on 'Why are ye subject to ordinances?' was –

From hence it has been inferred that Christians are not subject to the ordinances of Christ.

But with how little reason this has been inferred will sufficiently appear to all who consider: (1) That the ordinances here spoken of by St. Paul are evidently Jewish ordinances. (2) That, consequently, this has no reference to the ordinances of Christ, such as prayer, communicating, and searching the Scriptures. (3) That Christ himself spake that 'men' ought 'always to pray'; to search the Scriptures, and to eat bread and drink wine, in remembrance of him.

Friday, 27 June – I preached on 'Do this in remembrance of me.'

In the ancient church, every one who was baptized communicated daily. But in latter times many have affirmed that the Lord's Supper is not a converting, but a confirming ordinance.

But experience shows the gross falsehood of that assertion. Many now present know, the very beginning of your conversion to God (perhaps, in some, the first deep conviction) was wrought at the Lord's Supper. Now, one single instance of this kind overthrows the whole assertion.

Many then laboured to prove that my brother and I laid too much stress upon the ordinances.

One asked whether they would suffer Mr Wesley to preach at Fetter Lane. After a short debate it was answered, 'No; this place is taken for the Germans.' Some asked whether the Germans had converted any soul in England; whether they had not done us much hurt instead of good, and whether God did not many times use Mr Wesley for the healing of our divisions when we were all in confusion. Several roundly replied, 'Confusion! What do you mean? We were never in any confusion at all.'

We continued in useless debate till about eleven. I then gave them up to God.

Sunday, 20 July – At Mr Seward's earnest request, I preached once more in Moorfields, on the 'work of faith,' and the 'patience of hope,' and the 'labour of love.' A zealous man was so kind as to free us from most of the noisy, careless hearers (or spectators rather), by reading, meanwhile, at a small distance, a chapter in *The Whole Duty of Man*. I wish neither he nor they may ever read a worse book; though I can tell them of a better – the Bible.

In the evening I went to the lovefeast in Fetter Lane; at the conclusion of which, I read a paper, the substance whereof was as follows:

'About nine months ago certain of you began to speak contrary to the doctrine we had till then received. The sum of what you asserted is this:

1. That there is no such thing as *weak faith*.

2. That a man ought not to use those ordinances which our Church terms 'means of grace,' before he has such a faith as excludes all doubt and fear.

I believe these assertions to be flatly contrary to the Word of God. I have borne with you long, hoping you would turn. But as I find you more and more confirmed in the error of your ways, nothing now remains but that I should give you up to God. You that are of the same judgement, follow me.'

I then, without saying anything more, withdrew, as did eighteen or nineteen of the society.

Wednesday, 23 July – Our little company met at *The Foundery*, instead of Fetter Lane. About twenty-five of our brethren God hath given us already, all of whom think and speak the same thing; eight-and-forty likewise of the fifty women desired to cast in their lot with us.

Sunday, 17 August – I heard a sermon setting forth the *duty of getting a good estate*, and *keeping a good reputation*. Is it possible to deny that such a preacher is a 'blind leader of the blind?'

Thursday, 18 September – The prince of the air made another attempt in defence of his tottering kingdom. A great number of men, having got into the Foundery, began to speak big, swelling words; so that my voice could hardly be heard. But the hammer of the word brake the rocks in pieces; all quietly heard the glad tidings of salvation; and some, I trust, not in vain.

Tuesday, 25 November – After several methods proposed for employing those who were out of business, we determined to make a trial of one. Our aim was, with as little expense as possible, to keep them at once from want and from idleness; we took twelve of the poorest, and a teacher, into the society-room, where they were employed for four months, till spring came on, in carding and spinning of cotton. And the design answered; they were employed and maintained with very little more than the produce of their own labour.

Wednesday, 31 December – Many from Bristol came over to us, and our love was greatly confirmed toward each other. At half an hour after eight the house was filled from end to end, where we concluded the year, wrestling with God in prayer, and praising him for the wonderful work which he had already wrought upon earth.

1741

'Instead of doing as he had before proposed, he publicly put
me out by name, and though I sat with him at the desk, and
was a little surprised, yet I showed little of it to the souls, only
they saw me weep as I went out, for I said nothing.'
        John Cennick, Diary: 28 February 1741

Thursday, 1 January – [Bristol] I explained, 'If any man be in
Christ, he is a new creature.' But many of our brethren, I found,
had no ears to hear; having disputed away both their faith and
love.

Sunday, 1 February – [London] A private letter, wrote to me by
Mr Whitefield, having been printed without either his leave or
mine, great numbers of copies were given to our people, both at
the door and in the Foundery itself. Having procured one, I told
them, 'I will do just what I believe Mr Whitefield would were he
here himself.' Upon which I tore it in pieces before them all.
Every one who had received it did the same. So that in two minutes there was not a whole copy left.

Tuesday, 10 February – Before I began to preach, many men of
the baser sort, having mixed themselves with the women,
behaved so indecently as occasioned much disturbance. A
constable commanded them to keep the peace; in answer to
which they knocked him down. Some who were near seized on
two of them, and, shutting the doors, prevented any further
contest.

Saturday, 21 February – I inquired, as fully as I could, concerning the divisions and offences which began afresh to break out
in Kingswood.

Sunday, 22 February – Mr Cennick and fifteen or twenty others came up to me after sermon. I told them they had not done right in speaking against me behind my back.

In the evening there being mention made that many of our brethren at Kingswood had formed themselves into a separate society, I related to them at large the effects of the separations which had been made from time to time in London; and likewise the occasion of this, namely, Mr Cennick's preaching other doctrine than that they had before received.

Mr Cennick answered, 'You preach righteousness in man. I did say this; and I say it still. However, we are willing to join with you; but we will also meet apart from you.

I replied, 'You should have told me this before, and not have supplanted me in my own house, stealing the hearts of the people, by private accusations. He said, 'I have never privately accused you.' I said, 'My brethren, judge'; and read as follows: [letter by Cennick to George Whitefield, warning him of the Wesleys' attacks on Whitefield's teaching].

Mr Cennick stood up and said, 'That letter is mine, and I do not retract anything in it.'

Perceiving some of our brethren began to speak with warmth, I desired he would meet me on Saturday, where each of us could speak more freely, and that all things might sleep till then.

Saturday, 28 February – I met the Kingswood bands again, and I read the following paper: [announcement that certain members were expelled from the society, not for their opinions but for dissembling, lying etc].

At this they seemed a little shocked at first; but that they would not own they had done anything amiss.

I desired them to consider of it yet again the next evening.

Sunday, 1 March – They gave the same answer. However, I could not tell how to part; but exhorted them to wait yet a little longer.

Saturday, 7 March – The society being met together, I told them open dealing was best; and I would therefore tell them plainly what I thought had been wrong in many of them... and that we could not approve of delaying this matter.

Mr Cennick said, 'Unless in not speaking in your defence, I do not know that I have wronged you at all.'

I rejoined, 'It seems, then, nothing remains but for each to choose which society he pleases.'

Then, after a short time spent in prayer, Mr Cennick went out, and about half of those who were present, with him.

Sunday, 8 March – I earnestly besought them at Kingswood to beware of offending 'in tongue,' either against justice, mercy, or truth. The remains of our society met, and found we had great reason to bless God, for that, after fifty-two were withdrawn, we had still upwards of ninety left.

Saturday, 28 March – Having heard much of Mr Whitefield's unkind behaviour since his return from Georgia, I went to him to hear him speak for himself, that I might know how to judge. I much approved of his plainness of speech. He told me he and I preached two different gospels, and therefore he not only would not join with, or give me the right hand of fellowship, but was resolved publicly to preach against me and my brother.

Saturday, 4 April – I believed both love and justice required that I should speak my sentiments freely to Mr Whitefield concerning the letter he had published, said to be in answer to my sermon on Free Grace.

Tuesday, 14 April – I was much concerned for one of our sisters, who, having been but a few times with the 'still' brethren, was on a sudden so much wiser than her teachers that I could neither understand her, nor she me.

Tuesday, 21 April – I wrote to my brother: ['It is not possible for me to set out yet. I must go round and glean after Mr Whitefield. My journal is not written yet. The bands and society are my first care.

Send the new-printed Hymns immediately. We presented a thousand of Barclay to Mr Whitefield's congregation on Sunday.]

As yet I dare in no wise join with the Moravians: (1) Because their general scheme is mystical, not scriptural; (2) Because there is darkness and closeness in all their behaviour, and guile in almost all their words. (3) Because they utterly despise and decry self-denial. (4) Because they conform to the world, in wearing gold and costly apparel. (5) Because they are by no means zealous of good works, or at least only to their own people.'

Thursday, 7 May – I reminded the United Society that many of our brethren and sisters had not needful food; many were destitute of convenient clothing; many were out of business, and that without their own fault, and many sick and ready to perish; that I had done what in me lay to feed the hungry, to clothe the naked, to employ the poor, and to visit the sick; but was not, alone, sufficient for these things, and therefore desired all whose hearts were as my heart:

1. To bring what clothes each could spare, to be distributed among those that wanted most.

2. To give weekly a penny, or what they could afford, for the relief of the poor and sick.

My design, I told them, is to employ, for the present, all the women who are out of business, and desire it, in knitting.

Twelve persons are appointed to inspect these, and to visit and provide things needful for the sick.

Each of these is to visit all the sick within their district, every other day; and to meet on Tuesday evening, to give an account of what they have done, and consult what can be done farther.

Sunday, 10 May – I was obliged to lie down most of the day. In the evening my weakness was suspended while I was calling sinners to repentance. But at our lovefeast which followed, beside the pain in my back and head, and the fever which still continued upon me, I was seized with such a cough that I could hardly speak. At the same time came strongly into my mind 'These signs shall follow them that believe.' I called on Jesus aloud, to 'increase my faith', and to 'confirm the word of his grace.' While I was speaking, my pain vanished away, my bodily strength returned, and for many weeks I felt neither weakness nor pain. 'Unto thee, O Lord, do I give thanks.'

Monday, 8 June – For two days I had made an experiment which I had been often pressed to do; speaking to none concerning the things of God, unless my heart was free to it. And what was the event? Why, (1) That I spoke to none at all for four-score miles together; no, not even to him that travelled with me in the chaise, unless a few words at first setting out. (2) That I had no cross either to bear or to take up, and commonly in an hour or two fell fast asleep. (3) That I had much respect shown me wherever I came; every one behaving to me as to a civil, good-natured gentleman. Oh how pleasing is all this to flesh and blood! Need ye 'compass sea and land' to make 'proselytes' to this?

Thursday, 11 June – [Nottingham] At eight the society met as usual. I could not but observe – (1) That the room was not half full, which used to be crowded. (2) That not one person who came in used any prayer at all; but every one immediately sat down, and began either talking to his neighbour or looking about to see who was there. (3) That when I began to pray there appeared a general surprise, none offering to kneel down, and those who stood choosing the most easy, indolent posture which they conveniently could. I afterwards looked for one of our hymn-books upon the desk; but both that and the Bible were vanished away, and in the room lay the Moravian hymns and the Count's sermons.

Monday, 15 June – I set out for London, and read over in the way that celebrated book, Martin Luther's *Comment on the Epistle to the Galatians*. I was utterly ashamed. How have I esteemed this book, only because I heard it so commended by others; or, at best, because I had read some excellent sentences occasionally quoted from it! But what shall I say, now I judge for myself, now I see with my own eyes? Why, not only that the author makes nothing out, clears up not one considerable difficulty; that he is quite shallow in his remarks on many passages, and muddy and confused almost on all; but that he is deeply tinctured with mysticism throughout, and hence often dangerously wrong.

Here (I apprehended) is the real spring of the grand error of the Moravians. They follow Luther, for better, for worse. Hence their 'No works; no law; no commandments.' But who art thou that 'speakest evil of the law, and judgest the law?'

Saturday, 25 July – [Oxford] It being my turn (which comes about once in three years), I preached at St Mary's, before the University. So numerous a congregation (from whatever motives they came) I have seldom seen at Oxford. My text was the confession of poor Agrippa, 'Almost thou persuadest me to be a Christian.'

Tuesday, 25 August – I explained, at Chelsea, the nature and necessity of the new birth. One (who, I afterwards heard, was a Dissenting teacher) asked me when I had done, '*Quid est tibi nomen?*' [What is your name?] and, on my not answering, turned in triumph to his companions, and said, 'Aye, I told you he did not understand Latin!'

Tuesday, 1 September – I read over Mr Whitefield's account of God's dealings with his soul. Great part of this I know to be true. Oh 'let not mercy and truth forsake thee!'

Friday, 2 October – I preached at Cardiff, in the Shire Hall, on 'God hath given unto us eternal life, and this life is in his Son.' There having been a feast in the town that day, I believed it needful to add a few words upon intemperance: and while I was saying, 'As for you, drunkards, you have no part in this life; you choose death and hell,' a man cried out vehemently, 'I am one; and thither I am going.' But I trust God at that hour began to show him and others 'a more excellent way.'

Wednesday, 9 December – [Bristol] God humbled us in the evening by the loss of more than thirty of our little company, whom I was obliged to exclude, as no longer adorning the gospel of Christ. I believed it best openly to declare both their names and the reasons why they were excluded. We then all cried unto God that this might be for their edification, and not for destruction.

Friday, 11 December – I went to Bath. I had often reasoned with myself concerning this place, 'Hath God left himself without witness? Did he never raise up such as might be shining lights, even in the midst of this sinful generation? Doubtless he has; but they are either gone 'to the desert', or hid under the bushel of prudence. Some of the most serious persons I have known at Bath are either *solitary Christians*, scarce known to each other, or *prudent Christians*, as careful not to give offence as if that were the unpardonable sin.

1742

'My heart does not, and I am absolutely assured God does not, condemn me for any want of duty towards her in any kind, except only that I have not reproved her so plainly and fully as I should have done.'

John Wesley, letter to Charles Wesley, at the time of their mother's death.

Monday, 15 February – Many met together to consult on a proper method for discharging the public debt: and it was at length agreed, (1) that every member of the society who was able should contribute a penny a week; (2) that the whole society should be divided into little companies of classes – about twelve in each class; and (3) that one person in each class should receive the contribution of the rest, and bring it in to the stewards, weekly.

Sunday, 28 February – In the evening I set out for Wales.

Wednesday, 3 March – I rode to Llantrisant, and sent to the minister, to desire the use of his church. His answer was, the bishop had forbidden him. By what law? I am not legally convicted, either of heresy or any other crime. By what authority, then, am I suspended from preaching? By bare-faced arbitrary power.

Friday, 19 March – Pensford: The place where they desired me to preach was a little green spot near the town. I had no sooner begun than a great rabble came furiously upon us, bringing a bull, which they had been baiting, and now strove to drive in among the people. But the beast was wiser than his drivers; and, continually ran on one side of us or the other, while we quietly sang praise to God, and prayed for about an hour. The poor wretches at length seized upon the bull, now weak and tired, after having been so long torn and beaten, both by dogs and men; and, by main strength, partly dragged and partly thrust him in among the people. When they had forced their way to the little table on which I stood, they strove several times to throw it down, by thrusting the helpless beast against it. I once or twice put aside his head with my hand, that the blood might not drop upon my clothes; intending to go on as soon as the hurry should be over. But, the table falling down, some of our friends caught me and carried me right away on their shoulders; while the rabble wreaked their vengeance on the table. We went a little way off, where I finished my discourse without any noise or interruption.

Thursday, 25 March – [London] I appointed several earnest and sensible men to meet me, to whom I showed the great difficulty I had long found of knowing the people who desired to be under my care. After much discourse, they all agreed to divide them into classes, like those at Bristol, under the inspection of those in whom I could most confide. This was the origin of our classes at London, for which I can never sufficiently praise God, the unspeakable usefulness of the institution having ever since been more and more manifest.

Friday, 9 April – We had the first watch-night in London. We commmonly choose for this solemn service the Friday night nearest the full moon, either before or after, that those of the congregation who live at a distance may have light to their several homes. The service begins at half an hour past eight, and continues till a little after midnight. We have often found a peculiar blessing at these seasons, perhaps in some measure owing to the silence of the night, particularly in singing the hymn, with which we commonly conclude:

> Hearken to the solemn voice,
>   The awful midnight cry!
> Waiting souls, rejoice, rejoice,
>   And feel the Bridegroom nigh.

Friday, 23 April – I spent an agreeable hour with Mr Whitefield. I believe he is sincere in all he says concerning his earnest desire of joining hand in hand with all that love the Lord Jesus Christ. But if (as some would persuade me) he is not, the loss is all on his own side. I am just as I was: I go on my way, whether he goes with me or stays behind.

Wednesday, 12 May – I waited on the Archbishop of Canterbury with Mr Whitefield, and again on Friday; as also on the Bishop of London. I trust if we should be called to appear before princes, we should not be ashamed.

Friday, 21 May – I overtook a serious man, with whom I immediately fell into conversation. He gave me to know what his opinions were; I said nothing to contradict them. But that did not content him; he was quite uneasy to know whether I held the doctrine of the decrees as he did; but I told him, 'We had better keep to practical things, lest we should be angry at one another.' And so we did for two miles, till he caught me unawares and dragged me into the dispute before I knew where I was. He then grew warmer and warmer; told me I was rotten at heart, and supposed I was one of John Wesley's followers. I told him, 'No, I am John Wesley himself.' Upon which he would gladly have run away. But, being the better mounted, I kept close to his side, and endeavoured to show him his heart, till we came into Northampton.

Thursday, 27 May – We came to Newcastle about six, and walked into the town. I was surprised: so much drunkenness, cursing, and swearing (even from the mouths of little children) do I never remember to have seen and heard before, in so small a compass of time. Surely this place is ripe for him who 'came not to call the righteous, but sinners to repentance.'

Sunday, 30 May – At seven I walked down to Sandgate, the poorest and most contemptible part of the town, and, standing at the end of the street with John Taylor, began to sing the hundredth Psalm. Three or four people came out to see what was the matter, who soon increased to four or five hundred. I suppose there might be twelve to fifteen hundred before I had done preaching; to whom I applied those solemn words: 'He was wounded for our transgressions, and by his stripes we are healed.'

Observing the people to stand gaping and staring upon me with the most profound astonishment, I told them, 'If you desire to know who I am, my name is John Wesley. At five in the evening, with God's help, I design to preach here again.'

At five the hill was covered from top to bottom. I never saw so large a number of people together, either in Moorfields or at Kennington Common. I knew it was not possible for the one half to hear, although my voice was then strong and clear; and I stood so as to have them all in view. After preaching the poor people were ready to tread me under-foot, out of pure love and kindness.

Saturday, 5 June – I rode for Epworth. Before we came thither, I made an end of Madame Guyon's *Short Method of Prayer*. Ah, my brethren! I can answer your riddle, now I have ploughed with your heifer. The very words I have so often heard some of you use are not your own, no more than they are God's. They are only retailed from this poor Quietist. Oh that ye knew how much God is wiser than man! Then would you drop Quietists and Mystics together, and keep to the plain, practical, written Word of God.

It being many years since I had been in Epworth, I went to an inn in the middle of the town, not knowing whether there were any left in it now who would not be ashamed of my acquaintance. But an old servant of my father's with two or three poor women, presently found me out. I asked her, 'Do you know any in Epworth who are in earnest to be saved?' She answered, 'I am, by the grace of God; and I know I am saved through faith.' I asked, 'Have you, then, the peace of God? Do you know that he has forgiven your sins?' She replied, 'I thank God, I know it well. And many here can say the same thing.'

Sunday, 6 June – A little before the service I went to Mr Romley, the curate, and offered to assist him either by preaching or reading prayers; but he did not care to accept of my assistance.

The church was exceeding full in the afternoon, a rumour being spread that I was to preach. But the sermon on 'Quench not the Spirit' was not suitable to the expectation of many of the hearers. Mr Romley told them one of the most dangerous ways of quenching the Spirit was by enthusiasm; and enlarged on the character of an enthusiast in a very florid and oratorical manner. After sermon John Taylor stood in the churchyard, and gave notice, as the people were coming out, 'Mr Wesley, not being permitted to preach in the church, designs to preach here at six o'clock.'

Accordingly I found such a congregation as I believe Epworth never saw before. I stood near the east end of the church, upon my father's tombstone, and cried, 'The kingdom of heaven is not meat and drink; but righteousness, and peace, and joy in the Holy Ghost.'

Monday, 7 June – At eight in the evening I stood again on my father's tomb (as I did every evening this week), and cried aloud to the earnestly attentive congregation, 'By grace are ye saved through faith.'

Wednesday, 9 June – I rode over to a neighbouring town to wait upon a Justice of Peace, before whom angry neighbours had carried a whole wagon-load of these new heretics. But when he asked what they had done there was a deep silence. At length one said, 'Why, they pretended to be better than other people; and, besides, they prayed from morning to night.' Mr. Stovin asked, 'But have they done nothing besides?' 'Yes, sir,' said an old man: 'an't please your worship, they have *converted* my wife. Till she went among them, she had such a tongue! And now she is as quiet as a lamb.' 'Carry them back, carry them back,' replied the Justice, 'and let them convert all the scolds in the town.'

Sunday, 13 June – At six I preached for the last time in Epworth churchyard to a vast multitude gathered together from all parts. I continued among them for near three hours; and yet we scarce knew how to part. Oh let none think his labour of love is lost because the fruit does not immediately appear! Near forty years did my father labour here, but he saw little fruit of all his labour. I took some pains among this people too, and my strength also seemed spent in vain; but now the fruit appeared.

Tuesday, 20 July – [London] I found my mother on the borders of eternity. But she had no doubt or fear; nor any desire but (as soon as God should call) 'to depart, and to be with Christ.'

Friday, 23 July – About three in the afternoon I sat down on the bedside. She was unable to speak, but, I believe, quite sensible. Her look was calm and serene, and her eyes fixed upward, while we commended her soul to God. Then, without any struggle, or sigh, the soul was set at liberty. We stood round the bed, and fulfilled her last request: 'Children, as soon as I am released, sing a psalm of praise to God.'

Sunday, 1 August – Almost an innumerable company of people being gathered together, about five in the afternoon I committed to the earth the body of my mother. It was one of the most solemn assemblies I ever saw, or expect to see on this side eternity.

Monday, 16 August – I read over that surprising book, *The Life of Ignatius Loyola*, surely one of the greatest men that ever was engaged in the support of so bad a cause!

Sunday, 12 September – I was desired to preach in the Great Gardens, lying between Whitechapel and Coverlet Fields, where I found a vast multitude gathered. Taking knowledge that a great part of them were little acquainted with the things of God, I called upon them in the words of our Lord, 'Repent ye, and believe the gospel.' Many of the beasts of the people laboured much to disturb those who were of a better mind. They threw whole showers of stones, one of which struck me just between the eyes: but I felt no pain; and, when I had wiped away the blood, went on testifying that God hath given to them that believe 'not the spirit of fear, but of power, and of love, and of a sound mind.'

Tuesday, 28 September – I came to Windsor. I was soon informed that a large number of the rabble had combined together, and declared there should be no preaching there that day. In order to make all sure they had provided gunpowder and other things some days before. But Burnham Fair coming between, they agreed to go thither first. Accordingly they bestowed a few of their crackers upon their brother-mob at Burnham. But these, not being Methodists, did not take it well, turned upon them, and gave them chase.

Sunday, 26 December – I took occasion to show the usual way of keeping these days holy, in honour of the birth of our Lord; namely, by an extraordinary degree of gluttony and drunkenness; by heathen, and worse than heathen, diversions (with strife, cursing, and blasphemy); and by dancing and card-playing, equally conducive to the glory of God. I then described the right way of keeping a day holy, by extraordinary prayer, public and private; by thanksgiving; by hearing and meditating on his word, and by talking of all his wondrous works.

1743

'My brother came, delivered out of the mouth of the lion. He *looked* like a soldier of Christ. His clothes were torn to tatters.'

Charles Wesley, *Journal*, 21 October 1743

Sunday, 2 January – [Epworth] I preached from my father's tomb, on Hebrews 8:11. Many asked if it would not be well, as it was sacrament Sunday, for them to receive it. I told them, 'By all means; but first ask the curate's leave.' One did so, to whom he said, 'Pray tell Mr Wesley I shall not give *him* the sacrament, for he is not *fit.*'

How wise a God is our God! There could not have been so fit a place under heaven, where this should befall me first as the place of my nativity, where I had so long 'lived a Pharisee'! It was also fit he who repelled me should be one who owed his all in this world to the tender love which my father had shown to his, as well as to himself.

Saturday, 12 March – [Newcastle] I observed the number of those who had left the society since December 30 was seventy-six:

Fourteen (chiefly Dissenters) said they left it because otherwise their ministers would not give them the sacrament.

Nine, because their husbands or wives were not willing they should stay in it.

Twelve, because their parents were not willing. Five, because their master or mistress would not let them come.

Seven, because their acquaintance persuaded them.

Five, because people said such bad things of the society.

Nine, because they would not be laughed at.

Three, because they would not lose the poor's allowance.

Three more, because they could not spare the time to come.

Two, because it was too far off.

One, because she was afraid of falling into fits.

One, because people were so rude in the street.

Two, because Thomas Naisbit was in the society...

The number of those who were expelled was sixty-four:

Two for cursing and swearing.

Two for habitual Sabbath-breaking.

Seventeen for drunkenness.

Two for retailing spiritous liquors.

Three for quarrelling and brawling.

One for beating his wife.

Three for habitual, wilful lying.

Four for railing and evil-speaking.

One for idleness and laziness. And,

Nine-and-twenty for lightness and carelessness.

Sunday, 13 March – I am more and more convinced that the devil himself desires nothing more than that the people should be half-awakened and then left to fall asleep again. Therefore I determine, by the grace of God, not to strike one stroke in any place where I cannot follow the blow.

Sunday, 29 May (being *Trinity Sunday*) – I began officiating at the chapel in West Street, near the Seven Dials. I preached on the Gospel for the day; and afterwards administered the Lord's Supper to some hundreds of communicants. I was a little afraid that my strength would not suffice, when a service of five hours (for it lasted from ten to three) was added to my usual employment. But God looked to that. I preached at the Great Gardens at five, to an immense congregation, on 'Ye must be born again.' Then the leaders met and after them the bands. At ten at night I was less weary than at six in the morning.

Monday, 22 August – I rode softly to Snow Hill, where, the saddle slipping quite upon my mare's neck, I fell over her head, and she ran back into Smithfield. Some boys caught her and brought her to me again, cursing and swearing all the way. I spoke plainly to them, and they promised to amend.

Friday, 26 August – I set out for Cornwall.

Sunday, 28 August – [Exeter] The sermon we heard at church was quite innocent of meaning; what that in the afternoon was I know not, for I could not hear a single sentence.

I went to the Castle, where were gathered together (as some imagined) half the grown persons in the city. So vast a congregation in that solemn amphitheatre! And all silent and still, while I explained that glorious truth, 'Happy are they whose iniquities are forgiven, and whose sins are covered.'

Monday, 29 August – About sunset we were in the middle of the first pathless moor beyond Launceston. About eight we were got quite out of the way; but we had not gone far before we heard Bodmin bell. Directed by this, we came to the town before nine.

Wednesday, 31 August – [St Ives] As we were going to church, a large company at the market-place welcomed us with a loud huzza: as harmless as the ditty sung under my window:

> Charles Wesley is come to town,
> To try if he can pull the churches down.

Sunday, 11 September – We went as far as we could go safely, toward the point of the rocks at the Land's End. It was an awful sight! But how will these melt away when God ariseth to judgement! The sea between does indeed 'boil like a pot.'

Tuesday, 20 September – We reached Gwennap a little before six. It was supposed there were ten thousand people; to whom I preached Christ. I could not conclude till it was so dark we could scarce see one another. And there was on all sides the deepest attention, none speaking, stirring, or scarce looking aside. Surely here, though in a temple not made with hands, was God worshipped in 'the beauty of holiness'.

Thursday, 20 October – I rode to Wednesbury. I preached near the middle of the town to a far larger congregation than was expected. I believe every one felt the power of God; and no creature offered to molest us.

In the afternoon the cry arose that the mob had beset the house. We prayed that God would disperse them, and it was so. I told our brethren, 'Now is the time for us to go': but they pressed me exceedingly to stay. Before five the mob surrounded the house again in greater numbers than ever. The cry of one and all was, 'Bring out the minister; we will have the minister.' I desired one to take their captain by the hand and bring him into the house. After a few sentences interchanged between us the lion was become a lamb. I desired him to bring one or two of the most angry of his companions. He brought in two; in two minutes they were as calm as he. I then bade them make way, that I might go out among the people. I called for a chair, and, standing up, asked, 'What do any of you want with me?' Some said, 'We want you to go with us to the Justice.' I asked, 'Shall we go to-night, or in the morning?' Most of them cried, 'To-night'; on which I went before, and two or three hundred followed.

The night came on before we had walked a mile, together with heavy rain. However, on we went; one or two ran before to tell Mr Lane they had brought Mr Wesley before his Worship. Mr Lane replied, 'What have I to do with Mr Wesley? Go and carry him back again.' By this time the main body came up, and began knocking at the door. A servant told them Mr Lane was in bed. His son asked what was the matter. One replied, 'Why an't please you, they sing psalms all day; and make folks rise at five in the morning. What would your Worship advise us to do?' 'Go home,' said Mr Lane, 'and be quiet.'

Here they were at a full stop till one advised to go to Justice Persehouse at Walsall. All agreed; about seven came to his house. But Mr Persehouse likewise sent word that he was in bed. At last they all thought it the wisest course to make their way home. But we had not gone a hundred yards when the mob of Walsall came, pouring in like a flood, and bore down all before them.

To attempt speaking was vain, for the noise was like the roaring of the sea. So they dragged me along till, seeing the door of a large house open, I attempted to go in; but a man, catching me by the hair, pulled me back into the middle of the mob. They carried me through the main street, from one end of the town to the other. I continued speaking all the time to those within hearing, feeling no pain or weariness. At the west end of the town, seeing a door half open, I made toward it, but a gentleman in the shop would not suffer me, saying they would pull the house down. However, I stood at the door and asked, 'Are you willing to hear me speak?' Many cried out, 'No, no! knock his brains out; kill him at once.' Others said, 'Nay, but we will hear him first.' I began asking, 'What evil have I done? Which of you all have I wronged?' and continued speaking for above a quarter of an hour, till my voice suddenly failed. Then the floods began to lift up their voice again.

In the meantime my strength and my voice returned, and I broke out aloud into prayer. And now the man who just before headed the mob turned and said, 'Sir, I will spend my life for you: follow me, and not one soul here shall touch a hair of your head.' The people then, as if by common consent, fell back to the right and left; while three or four men took me between them, and carried me through them all. A little before ten, God brought me safe to Wednesbury, having lost only one flap of my waistcoat and a little skin from one of my hands.

From the beginning to the end I found the same presence of mind as if I had been sitting in my own study. I took no thought for one moment before another; only once it came into my mind that, if they should throw me into the river, it would spoil the papers that were in my pocket.

It ought not to be forgotten that, when the rest of the society made all haste to escape for their lives, four only would not stir – William Sitch, Edward Slater, John Griffiths, and Joan Parks; these kept with me, resolving to live or die together.

Tuesday, 25 October – [Grimsby] We were offered a very convenient place by a 'woman which was a sinner.' I there declared 'Him who God hath exalted, to give repentance and remission of sins.'

However, the prodigal held out till the evening, when I enlarged upon *her* sins and faith who 'washed our Lord's feet with tears, and wiped them with the hairs of her head.' She was then utterly broken in pieces, crying out, 'Oh, sir! "What must I do to be saved?"' I said, 'Escape for your life. Return instantly to your husband.' She said, 'But how can it be? He is above a hundred miles off at Newcastle-upon-Tyne.' I told her, 'I am going for Newcastle in the morning: you may go with me. William Blow shall take you behind him.' And so he did. Glory be to the Friend of sinners!

Sunday, 30 October – [Wensleydale] I showed, in the plainest words I could devise, that mere outside religion would not bring us to heaven; that none could go thither without inward holiness, which was only to be attained by faith. As I went back through the churchyard many were in high debate what religion this preacher was of. Some said, 'He must be a Quaker;' others, 'an Anabaptist.' But, at length, one deeper learned than the rest brought them all clearly over to his opinion, that he was a *Presbyterian-Papist*.

1744

'Ye venerable men who are more especially called to form
the tender minds of youth, are you filled with the Holy
Ghost?... How few of you spend, from one week to another,
a single hour in private prayer? How few of you have any
thought of God in the general tenour of your conversation?'

John Wesley, sermon before the University of Oxford,
24 August 1744

Wednesday, 15 February – [London] We were informed of the
invasion intended by the French, who were expected to land every
hour. I therefore exhorted the congregation, in the words of our
Lord, 'Watch ye therefore, and pray always, that ye may be
accounted worthy to escape all these things that shall come to
pass, and to stand before the Son of Man.'

We observed Friday the 17th as a day of solemn fasting and
prayer.

Saturday, 18 February – I received an account of another kind of
invasion in [Wednesbury,] Staffordshire. 'The mob had been
gathering all night, and on Tuesday morning they began their
work. They assaulted all the houses of those who were called
Methodists. They first broke all their windows, suffering neither
glass, lead, nor frames to remain. Then they made their way in;
and all the tables, chairs, chests of drawers, with whatever was not
easily removable, they dashed in pieces, particularly shop-goods,
and furniture of every kind. What they could not well break, as
feather-beds, they cut in pieces and strewed about the room.
William Sitch's wife was lying in; but that was all one; they pulled
away her bed too, and cut it in pieces. (Had the French come in

that place, would they have done more?) All this time none offered to resist them. Indeed most part, both men and women, fled for their lives...'

Thursday, 5 April – [St Ives] I took a view of the ruins of the house which the mob had pulled down, for joy that Admiral Matthews had beat the Spaniards. Such is the Cornish method of thanksgiving.

Wednesday, 11 April – I preached at Gwennap. I stood on the wall, in the calm, still evening, with the setting sun behind me, and almost an innumerable multitude before, behind, and on either hand. Many likewise sat on the little hills, at some distance. But they could all hear distinctly.

Monday, 16 April – Digory Isbel informed me of an accusation which I did not expect; no more than that other, vehemently asserted at St Ives, of my bringing the Pretender with me thither last autumn. It was that I called myself John Wesley; whereas everybody knew Mr Wesley was dead.

Monday, 23 April – I preached in the churchyard at Builth. I observed only one man with his hat on; probably through inattention; for he kneeled down on the grass with the rest as soon as I began to pray.

Tuesday, 24 April – I preached in Llanddwy church, near Brecknock. There was not a glass window belonging to it; but only boards, with holes bored here and there, through which a dim light glimmered in. Yet even here may the light of God's countenance shine. And it has shone on many hearts.

Monday, 14 May – [Sykehouse] Some affirmed that the mob was just a-coming, and that they would certainly fire the house or pull it down to the ground. I told them, then our only way was to make the best use of it while it was standing; so I began expounding the tenth chapter of St Matthew.

Monday, 1 June – I met John Nelson, at Durham, with Thomas Beard; another quiet and peaceable man, who had lately been torn from his trade, and wife and children, and sent away as a soldier; that is, banished from all that was near and dear to him, and constrained to dwell among lions, for no other crime, than that of calling sinners to repentance. His soul was in nothing terrified by his adversaries. Yet the body, after a while, sank under its burden. He was lodged in the hospital at Newcastle, where he still praised God continually. His fever increasing, he was let blood. His arm festered, mortified, and was cut off; two or three days after which God signed his discharge, and called him up to his eternal home.

Monday the 25th and the five following days we spent in conference [in London] with many of our brethren (come from several parts) who desire nothing but to save their own souls and those that hear them.

The next week we endeavoured to purge the society of all that did not walk according to the gospel. By this means we reduced the number of members to less than nineteen hundred. May God increase them in faith and love!

Friday, 24 August – [Oxford] I preached, I suppose the last time, at St Mary's. Be it so. I am now clear of the blood of these men. I have fully delivered my own soul.

The Beadle came to me afterwards and told me the Vice-Chancellor had sent him for my notes. I sent them without delay, not without admiring the wise providence of God. Perhaps few men of note would have given a sermon of mine the reading if I had put it into their hands; but by this means it came to be read by every man of eminence in the University!

Thursday, 27 December – I called on the solicitor whom I had employed in the suit lately commenced against me in Chancery; and here I first saw that foul monster, *a Chancery Bill*! A scroll of forty-two pages, in large folio, to tell a story which needed not to have taken up forty lines! And stuffed with such stupid, improbable lies (many of them too, quite foreign to the question) as, I believe, would have cost the compiler his life in any heathen court either of Greece or Rome. And this is *equity* in a Christian country!

1745

'Do you know the Wesleys? They make a great noise in the nation.'

'I know them well, King George; and thou mayest be assured that thou hast not two better men in thy dominions, nor men that love thee better than John and Charles Wesley.'

> George II, in a reported conversation with an eminent member of the Society of Friends at Kew.

Friday, 2 February – [riding to Newcastle] There was so much snow about Boroughbridge that we could go on but very slowly; insomuch that the night overtook us. But we pushed on at a venture across the moor, and, about eight, came safe to Sandhutton.

Saturday, 23 March – We found the roads abundantly worse, not only because the snows were deeper, which made the causeways in many places unpassable (and turnpike roads were not known in these parts of England till some years after), but likewise because the hard frost, succeeding the thaw, had made all the ground like glass. We were often obliged to walk, and our horses several times fell down while we were leading them. It was past eight before we got to Gateshead Fell, which appeared a great pathless waste of white. We were at a loss how to proceed, when an honest man of Newcastle overtook and guided us safe into the town.

Many a rough journey have I had before, but one like this I never had, between wind, hail, rain, ice, snow, sleet, and piercing cold. But it is past.

On Monday and Tuesday I diligently inquired who were offended at each other, this being the sin which most easily besets the people of Newcastle.

Wednesday, 27 March (being *Ash Wednesday*) – The little church in our house met together. Misunderstandings were cleared up, and we all agreed to set out anew, hand in hand, and, by the grace of God, to forward one another in running the race which is set before us.

Monday, 15 April – We met at half-hour past four, and the Room was filled from end to end. Many of the rich and honourable were there; so that I found it was time for me to fly away.

Sunday, 21 April – [Epworth] At five I preached at Mill Town. The poor miller near whose pond we stood endeavoured to drown my voice by letting out the water, which fell with a great noise. But it was labour lost; for my strength was so increased that I was heard to the very skirts of the congregation.

Thursday, 4 July – [West Cornwall] I was informed there were many here who had an earnest desire to hear 'this preaching,' but they did not dare, Sir Francis Vyvyan having solemnly declared, as they were coming out of church, 'If any man of this parish dares hear these fellows, he shall not – come to my Christmas-feast!'

Sunday, 7 July – Hearing the mob was rising again, I began preaching immediately. I had not spoke a quarter of an hour before they came in view. One Mr Trounce rode up first and began speaking to me, wherein he was roughly interrupted by his companions. Yet, as I stood on a high wall, and kept my eyes upon them, many grew calmer; which some of their champions observing, went round and suddenly pushed me down. I light upon my feet, without any hurt and, finding myself close the warmest of the horsemen, I took hold of his hand and held it fast while I expostulated the case. As for being convinced, he was quite above it: however, both he and his fellows grew much milder, and we parted very civily.

Monday, 9 September – I left London, and the next morning called on Dr Doddridge, at Northampton. It was about the hour when he was accustomed to expound a portion of Scripture to the young gentlemen under his care. He desired me to take his place. It may be the seed was not altogether sown in vain.

Tuesday, 17 September – [Osmotherley] I saw the poor remains of the old chapel, as well as those of the Carthusian monastery. The walls of the church, the cloister, and some of the cells are tolerably entire; and one may still discern the partitions between the little gardens, one of which belonged to every cell. Who knows but some of the poor, superstitious monks who once served God here according the light they had, may meet us, by-and-by, in that house of God 'not made with hands, eternal in the heavens?'

Wednesday, 18 September – About five we came to Newcastle, in an acceptable time. We found the generality of the inhabitants in the utmost consternation, news being just arrived, that, the morning before, at two o'clock, the Pretender had entered Edinburgh.

Thursday, 19 September – The mayor (Mr Ridley) summoned all the householders to the Town Hall; and desired as many as were willing to set their hands to a paper importing that they would, at the hazard of their goods and lives, defend the town against the common enemy. Fear and darkness were now on every side; but not on those who had seen the light of God's countenance.

Friday, 20 September – The mayor ordered the townsmen to be under arms, and to mount guard in their turns, over and above the guard of soldiers.

I had desired all our brethren to join with us in seeking God by fasting and prayer.

Saturday, 21 September – The same day the action was, came the news of General Cope's defeat. Orders were now given for the doubling of the guard, and for walling up Pandon and Sally-Port Gates.

Sunday, 22 September – The walls were mounted with cannon, and all things prepared for sustaining an assault. Meantime our poor neighbours, on either hand, were busy in removing their goods. And most of the best houses in our street were left without either furniture or inhabitants. More and more of the gentry every hour rode southward as fast as they could. At eight I preached at Gateshead, on the wisdom of God in governing the world. How do all things tend to the furtherance of the gospel!

All this week the alarms from the north continued, and the storm seemed nearer every day.

Sunday, 29 September – Advice came that they were in full march southward, so that it was supposed they would reach Newcastle by Monday evening. At eight I called on a multitude of sinners in Gateshead to seek the Lord while he might be found. In the afternoon we cried mightily to God to send his Majesty King George help from his holy place, and to spare a sinful land yet a little longer, if haply they might know the day of their visitation.

Wednesday, 9 October – It being supposed that the danger was over for the present, I preached at four in Gateshead.

Thursday, 10 October – We dined at Ferrybridge, where we were conducted to General Wentworth, who did us the honour to read over all the letters we had about us. We lay at Doncaster nothing pleased with the drunken, cursing, swearing soldiers who surrounded us on every side. Can these wretches succeed in anything they undertake? I fear not, if there be a God that judgeth the earth.

Monday, 4 November – I left Newcastle; we met several expresses sent to countermand the march of the army into Scotland, and to inform them that the rebels had passed the Tweed, and were marching southward.

Tuesday, 5 November – In the evening I came to Leeds, and found the town full of bonfires, and people shouting, firing of guns, cursing and swearing, as the English manner of keeping holidays is.

Saturday, 9 November – It was exceeding dark when I rode through Bilston. However, we did not stick fast till we came to Wednesbury town-end. Several coming with candles, I got out of the quagmire; and, leaving them to disengage my horse, walked to Francis Ward's house and preached.

Thursday, 28 November – I wrote *A Word to a Drunkard*.

Wednesday, 18 December – [London] Being the day of the National Fast, we met at four in the morning. I preached on Joel 2:12, etc. Abundance of people were at West Street chapel and at the Foundery, both morning and evening; as also (we understood) at every place of public worship throughout London and Westminster.

We had within a short time given away some thousands of little tracts among the common people. And it pleased God hereby to provoke others to jealousy. Insomuch that the Lord Mayor had ordered a large quantity of papers, dissuading from cursing and swearing, to be printed and distributed to the train-bands. And this day *An Earnest Exhortation to Serious Repentance* was given at every church door, in or near London, to every person who came out, and one left at the house of every householder who was absent from church.

Friday, 27 December – Having received a long letter from Mr Westley Hall, earnestly pressing my brother and me to renounce the Church of England (for not complying with which advice he soon renounced us), I wrote to him:

'Do you not here quite overlook one circumstance, which might be a key to our whole behaviour? Namely, that we no more look upon these filthy abuses which adhere to our Church as part of the building, than we look upon any filth which may adhere to the walls of Westminster Abbey as a part of that structure.'

1746

'I began my week's experiment of leaving off tea; but my flesh protested against it. I was but half awake and half alive all day; and my headache so increased toward noon, that I could neither speak nor think. So it was for the two following days, with the addition of a violent purging... This so weakened me, that I could hardly sit my horse.'

Charles Wesley, *Journal*, 28 July 1746

Tuesday, 18 February – [From Bristol to Newcastle] We pushed on through thick and thin, and with much difficulty got to Stanley. Thence, after an hour's stop, we hastened on. The brooks were so swoln with the late rains that the common roads were impassable; but our guide, knowing the country, carried us round about through the fields, so that we escaped the dangerous waters, and soon after sunset came (wet and dirty enough) to Evesham.

Thursday, 20 February – [Birmingham] We set out as soon as it was light. The rain changed into snow, which the northerly wind drove full in our faces, and crusted us over from head to foot in less than an hour's time. We inquired of one who lived at the entrance of the moors which was our best way to Stafford. 'Sir,' said he, ''tis a thousand pound to a penny that you do not come there to-day.' However, we went on, and I believe did not go ten yards out of the way till we came into Stafford. In the evening I preached and joined a few together as a society.

Saturday, 22 February – [Leeds] I preached at five. As we went home a great mob followed and threw whatever came to hand. I was struck several times, once or twice in the face, but not hurt at all.

Wednesday, 26 February – I came to Newcastle.

Friday, 23 May – I made over the houses in Bristol and Kingswood, and the next week that at Newcastle, to seven Trustees, reserving only to my brother and myself the liberty of preaching and lodging there.

Sunday, 6 July – After talking with the men and women leaders, we agreed it would prevent great expense, as well of health as of time and of money, if the poorer people of our society could be persuaded to leave off drinking of tea. We resolved ourselves to set the example. I expected some difficulty in breaking off a custom of six-and-twenty years' standing. And, the three first days my head ached, more or less, all day long, and I was half asleep from morning to night. The third day, my memory failed almost entirely. I sought my remedy in prayer. On Thursday morning my headache was gone; my memory was as strong as ever; and I have found no inconvenience, but a sensible benefit in several respects, from that very day to this.

Thursday, 17 July – I finished the little collection which I had made for a lending-stock: it did not amount to thirty pounds, which a few persons afterwards made up fifty. And by this inconsiderable sum above two hundred and fifty persons were relieved in one year.

Wednesday, 3 September – [Plymouth] Herbert Jenkins preached a plain, honest sermon; but the congregation was greatly displeased; and many went away as soon as he began, having come on purpose to hear me.

Friday, 26 September – [Wycombe] Mr B. went to the mayor, and said, 'Sir, I come to inform against a common swearer. I believe he swore an hundred oaths last night; but I marked down only twenty.' 'Sir,' said the mayor, 'you do very right in bringing him to justice. What is his name?' He replied, 'R– D–.' 'R– D–!'

answered the mayor; 'why, that is my son!' 'Yes, sir,' said Mr B., 'so I understand.' 'Nay, sir,' said he, 'I have nothing to say in his defence. If he breaks the law, he must take what follows.'

Thursday, 9 October – The day of Public Thanksgiving for the victory at Culloden was to us a day of solemn joy.

Wednesday, 12 November – In the evening, at the chapel, my teeth pained me much. In coming home, Mr Spear gave me an account of the rupture he had had for some years, which was perfectly cured in a moment. I prayed with submission to the will of God. My pain ceased, and returned no more.

Thursday, 4 December – I mentioned to the society my design of giving physic to the poor. About thirty came the next day, and in three weeks about three hundred. This we continued for several years, till, the number of patients still increasing, the expense was greater than we could bear. Meantime, through the blessing of God, many who had been ill for months or years were restored to perfect health.

Monday, 29 December – I resumed my vegetable diet (which I had now discontinued for several years), and found it of use both to my soul and body; but, after two years, a violent flux which seized me in Ireland obliged me to return to the use of animal food.

1747

'For natural sweetness of temper, for courtesy and hospitality, I have never seen any people like the Irish.'
John Wesley, letter 8 August 1747

Tuesday, 24 February – I examined the little society at Tetney. I have not seen such another in England. In the class-paper (which gives an account of the contribution for the poor) I observed one gave eight pence, often ten pence, a week; another thirteen, or eighteen pence; another, sometimes one, sometimes two shillings. I asked Micah Elmoor, the leader, 'How is this? Are you the richest society in all England?' He answered, 'I suppose not; but all of us who are single persons have agreed to give both ourselves and *all we have* to God. And we do it gladly; whereby we are able, from time to time, to entertain the strangers that come to Tetney, who often have no food to eat, nor any friend to give them a lodging.'

Friday, 13 March – In some of the following days I snatched a few hours to read *The History of the Puritans*. I stand in amaze: First, at the execrable spirit of persecution which drove those venerable men out of the Church, and with which Queen Elizabeth's clergy were as deeply tinctured as ever Queen Mary's were. Secondly, at the weakness of those holy confessors, many of whom spent so much of their time and strength in disputing about surplices and hoods, or kneeling at the Lord's Supper.

Tuesday, 30 June – We came to St Ives before morning prayers, and walked to church without so much as one huzza. How strangely has one year changed the scene in Cornwall! They give us good words almost in every place. What have we done, that the world should be so civil to us?

Wednesday, 1 July – I spoke severally to all those who had votes in the ensuing election. I found them such as I desired. Not one would even eat or drink at the expense of him for whom he voted.

Sunday, 2 August – I preached in Kingswood at eight, in the afternoon at Conham, and at five in the Old Orchard, to the largest congregation which I ever remember to have seen at Bristol. What hath God wrought in this city! And yet perhaps the hundredth part of his work does not now appear.

Saturday, 8 August – [Holyhead] Finding one of the packet-boats ready, we went on board about eight o'clock in the morning. It was a dead calm when we rowed out of the harbour; but about two in the afternoon the wind sprung up, and continued till near four on Sunday morning, when we were within sight of the Irish shore.

We came to St George's Quay [Dublin]. Soon after we landed, hearing the bells ringing for church, I went thither directly. About three I wrote a line to the curate of St Mary's, who sent me word he should be glad of my assistance: so I preached there (another gentleman reading prayers), to as gay and senseless a congregation as ever I saw.

Monday, 10 August – I met the society at five, and at six preached on 'Repent, and believe the gospel.' The room, large as it was, would not contain the people, who all seemed to taste the good word.

Tuesday, 11 August – I waited on the Archbishop at Newbridge, ten miles from Dublin. I had the favour of conversing with him two or three hours, in which I answered abundance of objections.

Friday, 14 August – I procured a genuine account of the great Irish massacre in 1641. Surely never was there such a transaction before, from the beginning of the world! More than two hundred thousand men, women, and children butchered within a few months, with such circumstances of cruelty as make one's blood run cold! It is well if God has not a controversy with the nation, on this very account, to this day.

Saturday, 15 August – I stayed at home, and spoke to all that came; but I found scarce any Irish among them. At least ninety-nine in an hundred of the native Irish remain in the religion of their forefathers. The Protestants, whether in Dublin or elsewhere, are almost all transplanted lately from England. Nor is it any wonder that those who are born Papists generally live and die such, when the Protestants can find no better ways to convert them than Penal Laws and Acts of Parliament.

Monday, 17 August – I began examining the society. It contained about two hundred and four score members, many of whom appeared to be strong in faith. The people in general are of a more teachable spirit than in most parts of England; but, on that very account, they must be watched over with the more care, being equally susceptible of good and ill impressions.

Wednesday, 2 September – [Cardiff] I spent some time with T. Prosser, who had filled the society with vain janglings. I found the fault lay in his head, rather than his heart. He is an honest, well-meaning man; but no more qualified, either by nature or grace, to expound Scripture than to read lectures in logic or algebra.

Friday, 16 October – [London] I went with two or three friends to see what are called the electrical experiments. How must these also confound those poor half-thinkers who will believe nothing but what they can comprehend! Who can comprehend how fire lives in water, and passes through it more freely than through air? How flame issues out of my finger, real flame, such as sets fire to spirits of wine? How these, and many more as strange phenomena, arose from the turning round a glass globe? It is all mystery; if haply by any means God may hide pride from man!

Friday, 25 December – We met at four, and solemnly rejoiced in God our Saviour. I found much revival in my own soul this day, and so did many others also. Both this and the following days I strongly urged the wholly giving up ourselves to God, and renewing in every point our covenant that the Lord should be our God.

1748

'The young preachers are for forcing my Brother to turn
Dissenter; that is, to go out like the snuff of a candle.'
Charles Wesley, letter to George Whitefield,
December 1763

Saturday, 16 January – Upon reviewing the account of the sick, we
found great reason to praise God. Within the year three hundred
persons had received medicines occasionally. About one hundred
had regularly taken them, and submitted to a proper regimen;
more than ninety of these were entirely cured of diseases they
had long laboured under.

Friday, 12 February – [Shepton Mallet] I found them all under a
strange consternation. A mob, they said, was hired, prepared,
and made sufficiently drunk in order to do all manner of mischief.
They attended us from the preaching-house, throwing dirt,
stones, and clods in abundance; but they could not hurt us. After
we were gone in to the house they began throwing great stones, in
order to break the door. Exactly while they burst in at one door,
we walked out at the other.

They filled the house at once, and proposed setting it on fire;
but one of them, happening to remember that his own house was
next, with much ado persuaded them not to do it.

Saturday, 27 February – [Holyhead] Mr Swindells informed me
that Mr Ellis would take it a favour if I would write some little
thing to advise the Methodists not to leave the Church, and not to
rail at their minister. I sat down immediately and wrote *A Word to
a Methodist*, which Mr Ellis translated into Welsh, and printed.

Sunday, 6 March – We went to Llangefni church, though we understood little of what we heard. Oh what a heavy curse was the Confusion of Tongues! And how grievous are the effects of it! All the birds of the air, all the beasts of the field, understand the language of their own species. Man only is a *barbarian* to man, unintelligible to his own brethren!

Wednesday, 16 March – [Dublin] I inquired into the state of the society. Most pompous accounts had been sent me, from time to time, of the great numbers that were added to it; so that I confidently expected to find six or seven hundred members. And how is the real fact? I left three hundred and ninety-four, and I doubt if there are now three hundred and ninety-six!

Let this be a warning to us all how we give in to that hateful custom of painting things beyond the life. Let us make a conscience of magnifying or exaggerating anything. Let us rather speak under than above the truth.

Sunday, 10 April – (*Easter Day*) Never was such a congregation seen before at the sacrament in Athlone. Abundance of Papists flocked to hear, so that the priest, seeing his command did not avail, came in person at six, and drove them away before him like a flock of sheep.

Tuesday, 12 April – I took my leave of the loving people, the like to whom I have never seen either in Europe or America. I believe more than an hundred followed me on foot above a mile to the top of the hill, and horsemen in abundance. We stopped here and sang the parting hymn, men, women, and children being in tears. I rode to Clara, where there was to begin, in an hour's time, a famous cockfight, to which almost all the country was coming from every side. Hoping to engage some part of them in a better employ, I began preaching in the street. One or two hundred stopped and listened a while, and pulled off their hats, and forgot their diversion.

Tuesday, 26 April – I read what is accounted the most correct history of St Patrick that is extant; and, on the maturest consideration, I was much inclined to believe that St Patrick and

St George were of one family. The whole story smells strong of romance.

Thursday, 5 May – Though my flux continually increased (which was caused by my eating a bad egg at Birr), yet I was unwilling to break my word, and so made shift to ride to Mountmellick.

Friday, 6 May – More people came at five than I had seen at that hour in any part of Ireland.

Tuesday, 10 May – With much difficulty I broke away from this immeasurably loving people.

Sunday, 15 May – [Dublin] I preached on Oxmantown Green. One, after listening some time, cried out, shaking his head, 'Aye, he is a Jesuit; that's plain.' To which a Popish priest, who happened to be near, replied aloud, 'No, he is not; I would to God he was.'

Friday the 24th June, the day we had appointed for opening the school at Kingswood, I preached there on 'Train up a child in the way that he should go; and when he is old, he will not depart from it.' My brother and I administered the Lord's Supper to many who came from far. We then agreed on the general rules of the school.

Friday, 12 August – In riding to Newcastle I finished the tenth Iliad of Homer. What an amazing genius had this man, to write with such strength of thought and beauty of expression, when he had none to go before him! And what a vein of piety runs through his whole work, in spite of his Pagan prejudices! Yet one cannot but observe such improprieties intermixed as are shocking to the last degree.

And what can be said for a king, full of days and wisdom, telling Achilles how often he had given him wine, when he was a child and sat in his lap, till he had vomited it up on his clothes?

Sunday, 28 August – I wonder at those who still talk so loud of the indecency of field-preaching. The highest indecency is in St

Paul's Church, when a considerable part of the congregation are asleep, or talking, or looking about, not minding a word the preacher says.

Thursday, 13 October – I preached in Bath at noon to many more than the room would contain. In the evening I preached in the street at Westbury, under Salisbury Plain. The whole congregation behaved well, though it was a town noted for rough and turbulent people.

Saturday, 22 October – I spent an hour in observing the various works of God in the Physic Garden at Chelsea. It would be a noble improvement of the design if some able and industrious person were to make a full and accurate inquiry into the use and virtues of all these plants. Without this, what end does the heaping them thus together answer, but the gratifying an idle curiousity?

1749

'Didst thou not make us one,
  That we might one remain,
Together travel on,
  And bear each other's pain,
Till all thy utmost goodness prove
And rise renewed in perfect love?'
          Charles Wesley, written during his courtship

Thursday, 6 April – [near Llantrisant] We rode to a hard-named place on the top of a mountain. I scarce saw any house near. However, a large number of honest, simple people soon came together; but few could understand me; so Henry Lloyd, when I had done, repeated the substance of my sermon in Welsh. The behaviour of the people recompensed us for our labour in climbing up to them.

About noon we came to Aberdare, just as the bell was ringing for a burial. This had brought a great number together, to whom, after the burial, I preached in the church.

Friday, 7 April – We reached Garth [Breconshire; the Gwynne family home].

Saturday, 8 April – I married my brother and Sarah Gwynne. It was a solemn day, such as became the dignity of a Christian marriage.

Monday, 24 April – The cold which I had had for some days growing worse and worse, and the swelling which began in my cheek increasing greatly, and paining me much, I sent for Dr

Rutty. But, in the meantime, I applied boiled nettles, which took away the pain in a moment. Afterwards I used warm treacle, which so abated the swelling that before the doctor came I was almost well.

Monday, 19 June – [Castlegar, Ireland] I had much conversation with Mrs M–, and was much in doubt, from the account she gave of her own experience, whether she had not been justified many years, though she knew it not by that name.

Sunday, 2 July – I preached at eight in Portarlington, and again at two. I scarce knew how to leave off; all the people seemed to be so deeply affected. In one week the face of the whole town is changed. Open wickedness is not seen; the fear of God is on every side; and rich and poor ask, 'what must I do to be saved?'

Wednesday, 19 July – I finished the translation of Martin Luther's *Life*. Doubtless he was a man highly favoured of God, and a blessed instrument in his hand. But oh, what a pity that he had no faithful friend – none that would, at all hazards, rebuke him plainly for his rough untractable spirit and bitter zeal for opinions.

Tuesday, 25 July – I rode over to Kingswood, and inquired particularly into the state of our school there. I was concerned to find that several of the Rules had been habitually neglected. I judged it necessary, therefore, to lessen the family – suffering none to remain therein who were not determined to observe them all.

Thursday, 27 July – I read Mr Law *On the Spirit of Prayer*. There are many masterly strokes therein, and the whole is lively and entertaining; but it is another gospel. For if God was never angry (as this tract asserts), he could never be reconciled; and, consequently, the whole Christian doctrine of reconciliation by Christ falls to the ground at once. An excellent method of converting Deists, by giving up the very essence of Christianity!

Saturday, 19 August – Twenty-eight depositions were laid before the Grand Jury at Cork; they threw them all out, and at the same time made that memorable presentment, which is worthy to be preserved in the annals of Ireland to all succeeding generations:

We find and present Charles Wesley [and others] to be a person of ill fame, a vagabond, and a common disturber of His Majesty's peace, and we pray he may be transported.

Friday, 22 September – [Whitehaven] I preached in the market-place, to a multitude of people, on 'Ye know the grace of our Lord Jesus Christ.' I saw they were moved, and resolved to improve the opportunity. So, after preaching, I desired those who determined to serve God to meet me apart from the great congregation. To these I explained the design, nature, and use of Christian societies.

At three in the afternoon I preached at Hensingham, a large colliery about a mile from the town. The eagerness of the people put me in mind of the early days at Kingswood. Oh why should we not be always what we were once?

Tuesday, 26 September – I had a solemn and delightful ride to Keswick, having my mind stayed on God.

Wednesday, 27 September – I took horse at half an hour past three. There was no moon or stars, but a thick mist, so that I could see neither road nor anything else. When I drew nigh Penruddock Moor the mist vanished, the stars appeared, and the morning dawned; so I imagined all the danger was past; but when I was on the middle of the moor, the mist fell again on every side, and I quickly lost my way. I lifted up my heart. Immediately it cleared up, and I soon recovered the high-road.

Friday, 29 September – I set out again for Whitehaven. The storm was exceeding high, and drove full in my face, so that it was not without difficulty I could sit my horse; particularly as I rode over the broad, bare backs of those enormous mountains.

About this time I was refreshed with a friendly letter from an excellent man whom I had not heard from for several years. [The letter, from John Boltzius in Georgia, then follows.] And yet this very man, when I was at Savannah, did I refuse to admit to the Lord's Table, because he was not baptized by a minister who had been episcopally ordained.

Can any one carry High Church zeal higher than this? And how well have I been since beaten with mine own staff!

Saturday, 9 December – I read the surprising *Extract of Mr Brainerd's Journal*. Surely, then, God hath once more 'given to the Gentiles repentance unto life!' Yet, amidst so great matter of joy, I could not but grieve at this: that even so good a man as Mr Brainerd should be 'wise above that is written,' in prescribing to God the way wherein he should work; and magnifying his own work, above that in Scotland, or among the English in New England: whereas, in truth, the work among the Indians, great as it was, was not to be compared to that at Cambuslang, Kilsyth, or Northampton.

1750

Monday, 22 January – I prayed in the morning at the Foundery,
and Howell Harris preached: a powerful orator, both by nature
and grace, but he owes nothing to art or education.

Sunday, 28 January – Mr Whitefield preached. How wise is God
in giving different talents to different preachers! Even the little
improprieties both of his language and manner were a means of
profiting many who would not have been touched by a more
correct discourse, or a more calm and regular manner of
speaking.

Monday, 29 January – I rode to Canterbury. The congregation in
the evening was deeply serious. I hope God will again have much
people in this place, who will worship him with more knowledge
and as much earnestness as their forefathers did the Virgin Mary,
or even St Thomas à Becket.

Thursday, 8 February – It was about a quarter after twelve that the
earthquake began. It went through Southwark, under the river,
and then from one end of London to the other. It was observed at
Westminster and Grosvenor Square a quarter before one. How
gently does God deal with this nation! Oh that our repentance
may prevent heavier marks of his displeasure!

Friday, 9 February – We had a comfortable watch-night at the chapel. About eleven o'clock it came into my mind that this was the very day and hour in which, forty years ago, I was taken out of the flames. I stopped and gave a short account of that wonderful providence. The voice of praise and thanksgiving went up on high, and great was our rejoicing before the Lord.

Thursday, 22 February – I went to see a young woman in Bedlam. But I had not talked with her long before one gave me to know that none of these preachers were to come there. So we are forbid to go to Newgate, for fear of making them wicked; and to Bedlam, for fear of driving them mad!

Sunday, 4 March – [Bristol] I desired John Whitford to preach at five; and I no longer wondered at the deadness of his hearers. I preached at Kingswood at eight, and God spoke to many hearts.

Sunday, 25 March – I preached at Howell Thomas', in Trefollwyn parish, to a small, earnest congregation. One of the brethren repeated the substance of the sermon in Welsh.

Wednesday, 28 March – [Holyhead] About eleven we were called to go on board. There was neither moon nor stars, but rain and wind enough. But we met another storm below, for who should be there but the famous Mr Griffith, of Carnarvonshire – a clumsy, overgrown, hard-faced man, whose countenance I could only compare to that (which I saw in Drury Lane thirty years ago) of one of the ruffians in *Macbeth*. I was going to lie down, when he tumbled in, and poured out such a volley of ribaldry, obscenity, and blasphemy, every second or third word being an oath, as was scarce ever heard at Billingsgate.

Monday, 30 April – [Mountmellick, Ireland] I administered the Lord's Supper to a sick person, with a few of our brethren and sisters. Being straitened for time, I used no extemporary prayer at all; yet the power of God was so unusually present during the whole time that several knew not how to contain themselves, being quite overwhelmed with joy and love.

Sunday, 13 May – I preached at Ahascragh to a congregation gathered from all parts. Oh what a harvest might be in Ireland did not the poor Protestants hate Christianity worse than either Popery or Heathenism!

Friday, 25 May – One Roger O'Ferrall fixed up an advertisement at the public Exchange that he was ready to head any mob in order to pull down any house that should dare to harbour a swaddler (a name give to Mr Cennick first by a Popish priest, who heard him speak of a child wrapped in swaddling clothes, and probably did not know the expression was in the Bible).

Wednesday, 15 August –I read over, with all the impartiality I could, the *Free and Candid Disquisitions*. With regard to the Common Prayer, even allowing all the blemishes to be real which he has so carefully and skilfully collected and recited, what ground have we to hope that if we gave up this we should profit by the exchange? Who would supply us with a Liturgy less exceptionable than that which we had before?

Monday, 3 September – [Shaftesbury] Soon after I was sat down, a constable came and said, 'Sir, the mayor discharges you from preaching in this borough any more.' I replied, 'While King George gives me leave to preach, I shall not ask leave of the mayor of Shaftesbury.'

Saturday, 15 September – I read over a short *Narrative of Count Zinzendorf's Life*, written by himself. Was there ever such a Proteus under the sun? For he has almost as many names as he has faces or shapes. Oh when will he learn (with all his learning) 'simplicity and godly sincerity? '

Monday, 3 December – I rode to Canterbury, and preached on Revelation 20. A few turbulent people made a little noise, as I found it was their custom to do.

Wednesday, 5 December – I walked over the cathedral, and surveyed the monuments of the ancient men of renown. One would think such a sight should strike an utter damp upon human vanity. What are the great, the fair, the valiant now? The matchless warrior, the puissant monarch? –

> A heap of dust is all remains of thee!
> 'Tis all thou art, and all the proud shall be.
>   [Pope]

1751

'Expenses on driving the Methodists: nine shillings.'
From the Church Accounts for the Parish of Illogan,
Cornwall

Wednesday, 30 January – [London] Having received a pressing letter from the Rector of our College, to give my vote at the election for a member of Parliament, which was to be the next day, I set out early, in a severe frost, with the north-west wind full in my face. The roads were so slippery that it was scarce possible for our horses to keep their feet. Nevertheless, God brought us safe to Oxford. A congregation was waiting for me at Mr Evans's, whom I immediately addressed in those awful words, 'What is a man profited, if he shall gain the whole world, and lose his own soul?'

Thursday, 31 January – I went to the schools, where the Convocation was met. The gentleman for whom I came to vote was not elected. Yet I did not repent of my coming.

Saturday, 2 February – Having received a full answer from Mr Perronet, I was clearly convinced that I ought to marry. For many years I remained single, because I believed I could be more useful in a single than in a married state. And I praise God, who enabled me so to do. I now as fully believed that in my present circumstances I might be more useful in a married state; into which, upon this clear conviction, and by the advice of my friends, I entered a few days after.

Wednesday, 6 February – I met the single men, and showed them on how many accounts it was good for those who had received that gift from God to remain 'single for the kingdom of heaven's sake'; unless where a particular case might be an exception to the general rule.

Sunday, 10 February – After preaching at five, I was hastening to take my leave of the congregation at Snowsfields; when, on the middle of London Bridge, both my feet slipped on the ice, and I fell with great force, the bone of my ankle lighting on the top of a stone. However, I got on, with some help, to the chapel. After preaching, I had my leg bound up by a surgeon, and made a shift to walk to the Seven Dials.

I went back in a coach to Mr B–'s, and from thence in a chair to the Foundery; but I was not able to preach, my sprain growing worse. I removed to Threadneedle Street, where I spent the remainder of the week.

[On 18 or 19 February, Wesley married Mrs Molly Vazeille.]

Wednesday, 27 March – I cannot understand how a Methodist preacher can answer it to God to preach one sermon or travel one day less in a married than in a single state.

Wednesday, 24 April – [Berwick-on-Tweed] Mr Hopper and I took horse between three and four, and about seven came to Old Camus. Whether the country was good or bad we could not see, having a thick mist all the way. The Scotch towns are like none which I ever saw. There is such an air of antiquity in them all, and such a peculiar oddness in their manner of building.

I had no intention to preach in Scotland, nor did I imagine there were any that desired I should. But I was mistaken.

Thursday, 25 April – We rode to Edinburgh; one of the dirtiest cities I had ever seen, not excepting Cologne in Germany.

Saturday, 11 May – We returned to Epworth, to a poor, dead, senseless people. At which I did not wonder when I was informed (1) that some of our preachers there had diligently gleaned up and retailed all the evil they could hear of me; (2) that some of them had quite laid aside our hymns, as well as the doctrine they formerly preached; (3) that one of them had frequently spoke against our rules, and the others quite neglected them.

Monday, 9 September – [Newlyn] About the middle of the sermon there was a vehement shower of rain and hail; but the bulk of the congregation stood quite still, every man in his place.

On Monday and Tuesday I preached in Ludgvan, Sithney, Crowan, and Illogan.

Friday, 13 September – I preached at St Mewan; Saturday the 14th at St Lawrence, near Bodmin: a little, ugly, dirty village. But I found God was there, even before I opened my mouth to a small, loving congregation.

Tuesday, 19 November – I began writing a letter to the Comparer of the Papists and Methodists [Dr Lavington]. Heavy work, such as I should never choose; but sometimes it must be done.

1752

'Love can bow down the stubborn neck
  The stone to flesh convert;
Soften, and melt, and pierce, and break
  the adamantine heart.

O that in me the sacred fire
  Might now begin to glow,
Burn up the dross of base desire,
  And make the mountains flow!'
  Charles Wesley, *Hymns and Sacred Poems*

Wednesday, 18 March – [Evesham] I saw Mr –'s aunt, who could not long forbear telling me how sorry she was that I should leave all my friends to lead this vagabond life. Why, indeed it is not pleasing to flesh and blood; and I would not do it if I did not believe there was another world.

Friday, 27 March (being *Good Friday*) – [Manchester] I went to the old church, where Mr Clayton read prayers; I think the most distinctly, solemnly, and gracefully of any man I have ever heard; and the behaviour of the whole congregation was serious and solemn in every part of the service.

Sunday, 5 April – [Birstall] Observing that several sat on the side of the opposite hill, I afterward desired one to measure the ground; and we found it was seven score yards from the place where I had stood. Yet the people there heard perfectly well. I did not think any human voice could have reached so far.

Friday, 24 April – [Hull] Clods and stones flew about on every side, but they neither touched nor disturbed me. When I had finished my discourse, I went to take coach; but the coachman had driven clear away. We were at a loss till a gentlewoman invited my wife and me to come into her coach. She brought some inconveniences on herself thereby, not only as there were nine of us in the coach, but also as the mob closely attended us, throwing in at the windows (which we did not think it prudent to shut) whatever came next to hand. But a large gentlewoman who sat in my lap screened me, so that nothing came near me.

Tuesday, 26 May – [Weardale] I had been out of order all night, and found myself now much weaker. However, I trusted in the Strong for strength, and began preaching to a numerous congregation.

In the evening we came to Allendale. My voice and strength were entirely restored, and I cried aloud, 'How shall I give thee up, Ephraim?' The mountains again flowed down at his presence, and the rocks were once more broken in pieces.

Monday, 15 June – I had many little trials of a kind I had not known before. I had borrowed a young, strong mare when I set out from Manchester; but she fell lame before I got to Grimsby. I procured another, but was dismounted again between Newcastle and Berwick. At my return to Manchester I took my own; but she had lamed herself in the pasture. I comforted myself that I had another at Manchester which I had lately bought; but I found one had borrowed her too, and rode her away to Chester.

Monday, 22 June – [Chester] We walked round the walls of the city, which are something more than a mile and three quarters in circumference; but there are many vacant spaces within the walls, many gardens, and a good deal of pasture ground.

The greatest convenience here is what they call 'the Rows'; that is, covered galleries, which run through the main streets on each side, from east to west, and from north to south, by which means one may walk both clean and dry in any weather from one end of the city to the other.

Saturday, 8 August – [Athlone] I called on a lively man, who is just married in the ninety-second year of his age. He served as an officer both in King William's and Queen Anne's wars, and a year or two ago began to serve the Prince of Peace. He has all his faculties of body and mind entire, works in his garden some hours every day, and praises God who has prolonged his life to so good a purpose.

Thursday, 14 September – (So we must call it now, seeing the New Style now takes place.) I rode to the bog of Boira, where a great and effectual door is opened.

Friday, 13 October – I read over Pascal's *Thoughts*. What could possibly induce such a creature as Voltaire to give such an author as this a good word, unless it was that he once wrote a satire? And so his being a satirist might atone even for his being a Christian.

Saturday, 14 October – I now rested a week at Bristol and Kingswood, preaching only morning and evening.

Sunday, 22 October – Having heard grievous complaints of the society in Kingswood, as if there were many disorderly walkers therein, I made a particular inquiry, and I found there was one member who drank too much in January or February last.

1753

'As you have made a pretty considerable progress in the mysteries of electricity, I would now humbly recommend to your diligent unprejudiced pursuit and study the mystery of the new birth. It is a most important, interesting study, and when mastered, will richly repay you for all your pains.'

George Whitefield, letter to his friend Benjamin Franklin, 14 August 1753

Saturday, 3 February – I visited one in the Marshalsea Prison – a nursery of all manner of wickedness. Oh shame to man that there should be such a place, such a picture of hell upon earth! And shame to those who bear the name of Christ that there should need any prison at all in Christendom!

Saturday, 17 February – From Dr Franklin's *Letters* I learned (1) that electrical fire (or ether) is a species of fire, infinitely finer than any other yet known; (2) that it is diffused, and in nearly equal proportions, through almost all substances... (4) that if any quantity of it be collected together, whether by art or nature, it then becomes visible in the form of fire, and inexpressibly powerful... What an amazing scene is here opened for after-ages to improve upon!

Monday, 5 March – [Bristol] I called on Mr Farley, and saw a plain confutation of that vulgar error that consumptions are not catching. He caught the consumption from his son, whereby he soon followed him to the grave.

Tuesday, 20 March – I preached in the town hall at Evesham. At the upper end of the room a large body of people were still and attentive. Meantime, at the lower end, many were walking to and fro, laughing and talking, as if they had been in Westminster Abbey.

Saturday, 31 March – I preached at Booth Bank, where I met Mr Cross, late gardener to the Earl of Warrington. Is it possible the Earl should turn off an honest, diligent, well-tried servant, who had been in the family above fifty years, for no other fault than hearing the Methodists?

Monday, 2 April – [Daveyhulme] I found (what I had never heard of in England) a whole clan of infidel peasants. A neighbouring alehouse-keeper drinks, and laughs, and argues into Deism all the ploughmen and dairymen he can light on. But no mob rises against him; Satan is not divided against himself.

Monday, 9 April – [Kendal] I preached in a large, convenient room. I was a little disgusted at their manner of coming and sitting down, without any pretence to any previous prayer; as well as at their sitting during the hymn, which indeed not one sung with me. But it was far otherwise after sermon, for God spake in his word.

Wednesday, 18 April – [Glasgow] I walked over the city. The students wear scarlet gowns, reaching only to their knees. Most I saw were very dirty, some very ragged, and all of very coarse cloth. The high church is a fine building, but it is miserably defaced within, having no form, beauty or symmetry left.

Friday, 4 May – We had the first General Quarterly Meeting of all the stewards round Newcastle, in order thoroughly to understand both the spiritual and temporal state of every society.

Sunday, 8 July – [Portsmouth] I was surprised to find so little fruit here, after so much preaching. That accursed itch of disputing had wellnigh destroyed all the seed which had been sown. And this 'vain jangling' they called 'contending for the faith.'

We took a walk round the town, which is regularly fortified, and is, I suppose, the only regular fortification in Great Britain or Ireland. Gosport, Portsmouth, and the Common (which is now all turned into streets), may probably contain half as many people as Bristol; and so civil a people I never saw before in any seaport town in England.

I went on board a hoy, and in three hours landed at Cowes, in the Isle of Wight: as far exceeding the Isle of Anglesey, both in pleasantness and fruitfulness, as that exceeds the rocks of Scilly.

We rode straight to Newport, the chief town in the Isle, and found a little society in tolerable order.

I walked to Carisbrooke Castle; or rather, the poor remains of it. It stands upon a solid rock on the top of a hill, and commands a beautiful prospect. There is a well, cut quite through the rock, said to be seventy-two yards deep; and another in the citadel, near a hundred. They drew up the water by an ass, which they assured us was sixty years old, but all the stately apartments lie in ruins. Only just enough of them is left to show the chamber where poor King Charles was confined, and the window through which he attempted to escape.

Wednesday, 25 July – The stewards met at St Ives from the western part of Cornwall. The next day I began examining the society, but I was soon obliged to stop short. I found an accursed thing among them: wellnigh one and all had bought or sold uncustomed goods. I therefore delayed speaking to any more till I had met them all together. In the evening I told them they must put this abomination away, or they would see my face no more.

Friday, 24 August – I endeavoured once more to bring Kingswood School into order. Surely the importance of this design is apparent, even from the difficulties that attend it. I have spent more money and time and care on this than almost any design I ever had; and still it exercises all the patience I have. But it is worth all the labour.

Wednesday, 3 October – [Shorwell, Isle of Wight] I preached to all the poor and middling people of the town. I believe some of the rich also designed to come, but something of more importance – a dinner – came between.

Sunday, 7 November – [Portsmouth] I explained the nature and design of our societies. I made no account of that shadow of a society which was before, without classes, order or rules, having never seen, read or heard the printed rules which ought to have been given them at their very first meeting.

Monday, 26 November – [London] Dr Fothergill told me plain, I must not stay in town a day longer; adding, 'If anything does thee good, it must be the country air, with rest, asses' milk, and riding daily.' So, (not being able to sit a horse) about noon I took coach for Lewisham.

In the evening (not knowing how it might please God to dispose of me), to prevent vile panegyric, I wrote as follows:

> Here lieth the Body
> of
> John Wesley
> A brand plucked out of the burning:
> who died of a consumption in the fifty-first year of his age,
> not leaving, after his debts are paid,
> ten pounds behind him:
> praying,
> God be merciful to me, an unprofitable servant!

Wednesday, 28 November – About noon (the time that some of our brethren had set apart for prayer) a thought came into my mind to make an experiment. So I ordered some stone brimstone to be powdered, mixed with the white of an egg, and spread on brown paper, which I applied to my side. The pain ceased in five minutes, the fever in half an hour, and from this hour I began to recover. The next day I was able to ride, which I continued till January 1.

1754

'Ephesians 2:8 *By grace are ye saved through faith* – Grace, without any respect to human worthiness, conveys the glorious gift. Faith, with an empty hand, and without any pretence of personal desert, receives the heavenly blessing... 1 John 4:19 *We love him, because he first loved us* – This is the sum of all religion, the genuine model of Christianity. None can say more; why should any say less, or less intelligibly?'

      John Wesley, *Explanatory Notes upon the New Testament*

Friday, 4 January – [Bristol] I began drinking the water at the Hot Well, having a lodging at a small distance from it; and on Sunday the 6th I began writing *Notes on the New Testament* – a work which I should scarce ever have attempted had I not been so ill as not to be able to travel or preach.

Wednesday, 13 February – I was sent for by one dying of a consumption. She seemed full of good desires: but who does not, when death stands at the door?

Monday, 29 April – I preached at Sadler's Wells, in what was formerly a play-house. I am glad when it pleases God to take possession of what Satan esteemed his own ground.

Sunday, 2 June (being *Whit Sunday*) – I preached at the Foundery, which I had not done before in the evening. Still I have not recovered my whole voice or strength; perhaps I never may. But let me use what I have.

Thursday, 20 June – We spent some hours at Wrest, a seat of the late Duke of Kent, who was forty years laying out and improving the gardens. But how little rest did its miserable master enjoy! 'Thou, O God, hast made our heart for thyself, and it cannot rest till it resteth in thee.'

Monday, 5 August – I read Mr Baxter's *History of the Councils*. What a company of execrable wretches have they been who have almost in every age, since St Cyprian, taken upon them to govern the Church! Surely Mahometanism was let loose to reform the Christians!

Wednesday, 2 October – I walked to Old Sarum, which, in spite of common sense, without house or inhabitant, still sends two members to the Parliament. It is a large, round hill, encompassed with a broad ditch. Probably before the invention of cannon, this city was impregnable. Troy was; but now it is vanished away.

Monday, 7 October – I retired to a little place near Hackney, formerly a seat of Bishop Bonner's (how are the times changed!) and still bearing his name.

1755

'Me'thodist… (2) One of a new kind of puritans lately arisen, so called from their profession to live by rules and in constant method.'

Samuel Johnson, *A Dictionary of the English Language* 1755

Tuesday, 15 April – I went to Liverpool, one of the neatest, best-built towns I have seen in England. I think it is full twice as large as Chester. Two-thirds of the town have been added within these forty years. If it continue to increase in the same proportion, in forty years more it will nearly equal Bristol. The people in general are the most mild and courteous I ever saw in a seaport town; as indeed appears by their friendly behaviour, not only the Jews and Papists who live among them, but even to the Methodists (so called).

Sunday, 27 April – As I walked by, I saw a good old man bleeding almost to death. I desired him immediately to snuff vinegar up his nose, and apply it to his neck, face, and temples. It was done, and the blood entirely stopped in less than two minutes.

Wednesday, 30 April – [My brother and I] began reading together *A Gentleman's Reasons for his Dissent from the Church of England*. In how different a spirit does this man write from honest Richard Baxter! The one dipping, as it were, his pen in tears, the other in vinegar and gall. Surely one page of that loving, serious Christian weighs more than volumes of this bitter, sarcastic jester.

Tuesday, 6 May –Our Conference began at Leeds. The point on which we desired all the preachers to speak their minds was, 'Whether we ought to separate from the Church?' On the third day we were all fully agreed that (whether it was *lawful* or not) it was no ways *expedient*.

Sunday, 3 August – I dined with one who lived for many years with one of the most celebrated beauties in Europe. She was also proud, vain, and nice to a very uncommon degree. But see the end! After a painful and nauseous disease she rotted away above ground, and was so offensive for many days before she died that scarce any could bear to stay in the room.

Wednesday, 6 August – [London] I mentioned to the congregation another means of increasing serious religion, which had been frequently practised by our forefathers, namely, the joining in a covenant to serve God with all our heart and with all our soul. I explained this for several mornings following, and on Friday many of us kept a fast unto the Lord, beseeching him to give us wisdom and strength to promise unto the Lord our God and keep it.

Monday, 11 August – I explained once more the nature of such an engagement, and the manner of doing it acceptably to God. At six in the evening we met for that purpose at the French church in Spitalfields. After I had recited the tenor of the covenant, all the people stood up, in testimony of assent, to the number of about eighteen hundred persons. Such a night I scarce ever saw before. Surely the fruit of it shall remain for ever.

Sunday, 6 September – [St Just] Except at Gwennap, I have seen no such congregation in Cornwall. The sun shone full in my face when I began the hymn; but just as I ended it a cloud arose, which covered it till I had done preaching. Is anything too small for the providence of him by whom our very hairs are numbered?

Friday, 3 October – I rode over to Pill, a place famous from generation to generation, even as Kingswood itself, for stupid, brutal, abandoned wickedness. But what is all the power of the world and the devil, when the day of God's power is come?

Wednesday, 15 October – [Bristol] I had desired again and again that no person would come who had not calmly and deliberately resolved to give himself up to God. But I believe not ten of them were wanting, and we now solemnly and of set purpose, by our own free act and deed, jointly agreed to take the Lord for our God. I think it will not soon be forgotten; I hope not to all eternity.

Monday, 10 November – [London] The frost was very severe, accompanied with such a fog as perhaps the oldest man there never saw before. The lamps could not be seen across the street. Many lost their way when they were just at their own doors. And it was almost as hard to breathe as to see. How easy it is for God to punish a sinful nation!

Tuesday, 23 December – I was in the robe-chamber adjoining to the House of Lords when the King put on his robes. His brow was much furrowed with age, and quite clouded with care. And is this all the world can give even to a king? A blanket of ermine round his shoulders, so heavy and cumbersome he can scarce move under it! A huge heap of borrowed hair, with a few plates of gold and glittering stones upon his head! Alas, what a bauble is human greatness! And even this will not endure.

1756

Thursday, 1 January – We had a large congregation at four in the morning. How much are men divided in their expectations concerning the ensuing year! Will it bring a large harvest of temporal calamities, or of spiritual blessings?

Monday, 26 January – [Canterbury] I preached in the evening to such a congregation as I never saw there before, in which were abundance of the soldiers, and not a few of their officers.

Wednesday, 3 March – I found Bristol all in a flame, voters and non-voters being ready to tear each other in pieces. I desired those members who were freemen to meet me by themselves, whom I mildly and lovingly informed how they ought to act in this hour of temptation.

Thursday, 1 April – [Dublin] I bought one or two books at Mr Smith's on the Blind Quay. I wanted change for a guinea, but he could not give it, so I borrowed some silver of my companion. The next evening a young gentleman came from Mr Smith's to tell me I had left a guinea on his counter. Such an instance of honesty I have rarely met with.

Sunday, 4 April – I went to the college chapel, at which about forty persons were present. Dr Knight preached a plain, practical sermon, after which the sacrament was administered. I never saw so much decency at any chapel in Oxford, no, not even at Lincoln College. Scarce any person stirred or coughed or spit from the beginning to the end.

Friday, 16 April (being *Good Friday*) – Near four hundred of the society met, to follow the example of their brethren in England, and renew their covenant with God.

Wednesday, 19 May – [Cork] While I was speaking, a gentleman in the gallery cried out, 'I am of the Church; I stand up for the Church; I will shed my blood for the Church.' But, finding none to contradict him, he sat down.

Friday, 16 July – About this time I received a letter without a name, part of which I have subjoined:
Sir,
   Having observed your labours of love for the common people, I presume to beg your pen in behalf of the next class of God's creatures.
   I am persuaded you are not insensible of the pain given to every Christian, every humane heart, by those savage diversions, bull-baiting, cock-fighting, horse-racing, and hunting. Can any of these irrational and unnatural sports appear otherwise than cruel, unless through early prejudice or entire want of consideration and reflection? And, besides, how dreadful are the concomitant and the consequent vices of these savage routs! Yet such cowards are we grown that scarce any man has courage to draw his pen against them!

Friday, 23 July – [Lisburn] the rector, with his curate, called upon me, candidly proposed their objections, and spent about two hours in free, serious, friendly conversation. How much evil might be prevented or removed would other clergymen follow their example!
   We rode along the shore to Carrickfergus, said to be the most ancient town in Ulster. The walls are still, as it were, standing,

and the castle built upon a rock; but it is little more than a heap of ruins, with eight or nine old, dismounted, rusty cannon. What it was in the reign of its founder, King Fergus, does not much concern us to know.

Sunday, 25 July – At eleven I went to church, to the surprise of many, and heard a lively, useful sermon. After dinner one of our brethren asked if I was ready to go to meeting. I told him 'I never go to meeting.' He seemed as much astonished as the old Scot at Newcastle, who left us because we were mere Church of England men. We are so, although we condemn none who have been brought up in another way.

Monday, 26 July – I spoke very plain at Lisburn, both to the great vulgar and the small. But between Seceders, old self-conceited Presbyterians, New-Light men, Moravians, Cameronians, and formal Churchmen, it is a miracle of miracles if any here bring forth fruit to perfection.

Thursday, 12 August – [On the packet-boat to Holyhead] We began singing on the quarter-deck, which soon drew all our fellow passengers, as well as the captain, with the greatest part of his men. I afterwards gave an exhortation. We then spent some time in prayer. They all kneeled down with us; nor did their seriousness wear off all the day.

Saturday, 28 August – [Bristol] My brother and I closed the Conference by a solemn declaration of our purpose never to separate from the Church; and all our brethren concurred therein.

Monday, 11 October – I read over a curiosity indeed – a French heroic poem, Voltaire's *Henriade*. I was more than ever convinced that the French is the poorest, meanest language in Europe; that it is no more comparable to the German or Spanish than a bag-pipe is to an organ; and that, considering the incorrigible uncouthness of their measure, and their always writing in rhymes (to say nothing of their vile double rhymes, nay, and frequent false rhymes), it is as impossible to write a fine poem in French as to make fine music upon a jew's-harp.

Wednesday, 20 October – I received the following letter:
Rev. Sir,
As it is our duty to do all we can to make all around us happy, I think there is one thing that may be done to promote so blessed an end; namely, to efface all the obscene words which are written on houses, doors, or walls by evil-minded men. This, which I recommend to others, I constantly practise myself. I do it with a sponge, which for that purpose I carry in my pocket. As all persons, especially the young, are liable to temptations to impurity, I cannot do too much to remove such temptations. Perhaps, when the unhappy writers pass by, and see their bad labours soon effaced, they may be discouraged from pursuing so shameful a work.

In some places it might not be amiss, in the room of what is effaced, to write some serious sentence, or short text of Scripture.

Monday, 1 November was a day of triumphant joy, as All-Saints' Day generally is. How superstitious are they who scruple giving God solemn thanks for the lives and deaths of his saints!

Tuesday, 9 November – Having procured an apparatus on purpose, I ordered several persons to be electrified, who were ill of various disorders; some of whom found an immediate, some a gradual cure.

1757

'*The Plague (To prevent)*
Eat Marigold Flowers daily, as a sallad, with Oil and Vinegar...
The Plague (To cure)
Cold water alone, drank largely, has cured it...
The Pleurisy
Take out the core of an Apple, fill it with white Frankincense; stop it close with the piece you cut out, and roast it in the ashes. Mash and eat it.

or,

A glass of Tar-water, warm, every half-hour;

or,

A decoction of Nettles; and apply the herb hot, as a poultis.

or,

A plaister of Flour of Brimstone and White of an egg.

or,

Apply to the side Onion, roasted in the embers, mixt with cream.'

John Wesley, in *Primitive Physick*, first published 1747

Thursday, 10 February – The more I consider them, the more I doubt of all systems of astronomy. I doubt whether we can certainly know either the distance or magnitude or any star in the firmament. Else why do astronomers so immensely differ, even with regard to the distance of the sun from the earth? – some affirming it to be only three, others ninety, millions of miles!

Wednesday, 16 February – Calling on a friend, I found him just seized with all the symptoms of a pleurisy. I advised him to apply a brimstone plaster, and in a few hours he was perfectly well.

Now to what end should this patient have taken a heap of drugs, and lost twenty ounces of blood? Why, to oblige the doctor and apothecary. Enough! Reason good!

Thursday, 28 May – I talked with one who, by the advice of his pastor, had, very calmly and deliberately, beat his wife with a large stick till she was black and blue almost from head to foot. And he insisted it was his duty so to do, because she was surly and ill-natured; and that he was full of faith all the time he was doing it, and had been so ever since.

Sunday, 24 July – [Haxey Car] I preached to the largest congregation I have seen since I left Newcastle. All behaved with deep seriousness but one man, whom I afterward learned to be a Baptist preacher. Just as I was taking horse he came again, and laboured hard to begin a dispute; but, having neither time nor strength to spare, I gave him the ground and rode away.

Monday, 25 July – [Clayworth] I think none was unmoved but Michael Fenwick, who fell fast asleep under an adjoining hayrick. [Michael Fenwick, a young Methodist, was upset because until now he had not been named in the *Journal*. This time Wesley met his wishes.]

Saturday, 24 September – I preached [at Mevagissey]. All the time I stayed the wind blew from the sea, so that no boat could stir out. By this means all the fishermen (who are the chief part of the town) had opportunity of hearing.

Sunday, 25 September – [St Austell] The whole church service was performed by a clergyman, above ninety years of age. Stephen Hugo has been vicar of St Austell between sixty and seventy years. Oh what might a man full of faith and zeal have done for God in such a course of time!

Tuesday, 25 October – A man met me near Hanham, and told me the school-house at Kingswood was burned down. I felt not one moment's pain, knowing that God does all things well. About eight on Monday evening two or three boys had gone into the gallery; one of them heard a strange crackling in the room above. Opening the stair-case door, he was beat back by smoke, on which he cried out, 'Fire! Fire!' Mr Baynes, hearing this, ran immediately down, and brought up a pail of water. But when he went into the room,and saw the blaze, he had not presence of mind to go up to it, but threw the water upon the floor.

However, John How (who lived next door) ran up with an axe in his hand. He found the ladder was so short that, as he stood on the top of it, he could but just lay one hand over the battlements. How he got over none can tell, but he quickly broke through the roof, on which a vent being made, the smoke and flame issued out as from a furnace. Those who were at the foot of the stairs with water, then went through the smoke to the door of the leads, and poured it down through the tiling. By this means the fire was quickly quenched.

It is amazing that so little hurt was done. We observed Friday the 28th as a solemn fast; and from this time the work of God revived in Bristol.

Thursday, 3 November – [Pill] How is the face of things changed here! Such a sink of sin was scarce to be found; and now many are rejoicing in God their Saviour!

Monday, 7 November – Leaving the flame just kindling in Bristol, I rode to Newbury, and on Tuesday to London.

Monday, 5 December – I baptized Henrique Judah Seniore, a Portuguese Jew more than sixty years of age. He seemed to have no confidence in himself, but to be waiting for 'the consolation of Israel.'

1758

'Father of everlasting love,
    To every soul thy Son reveal,
Our guilt and suffering to remove,
    Our deep, original wound to heal,
And bid the fallen race arise,
And turn our earth to paradise.'
              Charles Wesley, *Hymns of Intercession* 1758

Monday, 9 January – [Bristol] I began a letter to Mr Towgood, author of *The Dissenting Gentleman's Reasons* – I think the most saucy and virulent satire on the Church of England that ever my eyes beheld. How much rather would I write practically than controversially! But even this talent I dare not bury in the earth.

Sunday, 2 April – [Dublin] The congregation was small. I took knowledge that the people had neither seen nor heard much of self-denial since T. Walsh left the kingdom.

Thursday, 20 April – In the evening I met all the married men and women of the society. I believe it was high time. For many of them seemed to know very little of relative duties: so that I brought strange things to their ears when I enlarged on the duties of husbands, and wives, and parents.

Friday, 21 April – I dined at Lady –'s. We need great grace to converse with great people! From which, therefore (unless in some rare instances), I am glad to be excused.

Wednesday, 24 May – I preached at Edgeworthstown to a very genteel congregation, extremely different from that which gathered at Longford, in the yard of the great inn – the rudest, surliest, wildest people that I have found since I came into the kingdom.

Thursday, 25 May – I rode to Drummersnave. Wood, water, fruitful land, and gently rising hills contribute to make this place a little paradise. Mr Campbell, the proprietor of the whole, resolved to make it such; so he planted groves, laid out walks, and formed the plan of a new town. But, alas! death stepped in between, and all his plan fell to the ground.

Sunday, 25 June – [Courtmatrix] I preached in a square green enclosure, which was formerly Oliver Cromwell's camp. To how much better purpose is this ground employed than it was in the last century!

Tuesday, 1 August – I learned two or three rules, very needful for those who sail between England and Ireland: (1) Never pay till you set sail; (2) Go not on board till the captain goes on board; (3) Send not your baggage on board till you go on yourself.

Thursday, 17 August – [Bristol] I went to the cathedral to hear Mr Handel's *Messiah*. I doubt if that congregation was ever so serious at a sermon as they were during this performance. In many parts, especially several of the choruses, it exceeded my expectation.

Friday, 6 October – I designed to go in a wherry to the Isle of Wight; but the watermen were so extravagant in their demands that I changed my mind, and went in the hoy. We landed at two, and walked on, five little miles, to Newport. The neighbouring camp had filled the town with soldiers, the most abandoned wretches whom I ever yet saw. Their whole glorying was in cursing, swearing, drunkenness, and lewdness. How gracious is God, that he does not yet send those monsters to their own place!

Sunday, 5 November – [Norwich] We went to St Peter's church, the Lord's Supper being administered there. I scarcely ever remember to have seen a more beautiful parish church; the more so because its beauty results not from foreign ornaments, but from the very form and structure of it. It is very large, and the sides are almost all window; so that it has an awful and venerable look, and, at the same time, surprisingly cheerful.

Wednesday, 29 November – [Wandsworth] I baptized two negroes belonging to Mr Gilbert, a gentleman lately come from Antigua. One is deeply convinced of sin, the other rejoices in God her Saviour, and is the first African Christian I have known. But shall not our Lord, in due time, have these heathens also 'for his inheritance?'

Monday, 4 December – I was desired to step into the little church behind the Mansion House, commonly called St Stephen's Walbrook. It is nothing grand, but neat and elegant beyond expression. I do not wonder at the speech of the famous Italian architect, who met Lord Burlington in Italy: 'My lord, go back and see St Stephen's in London. We have not so fine a piece of architecture in Rome.'

1759

'You totally lose my esteem; you violently shock my love; you quite destroy my confidence. You oblige me to lock up everything, as from a thief... You cut yourself off from joint prayer. For how can I pray with one that is daily watching to do me hurt?'

John Wesley, letter to his wife, November 1759

Wednesday, 21 March – [Colchester] I baptized seven adults, two of them by immersion; and in the evening (their own ministers having cast them out for going to hear the Methodists) I administered the Lord's Supper to them, and many others, whom their several teachers had repelled for the same reason.

Sunday, 1 April – [Norwich] I met them all at six, requiring every one to show his ticket when he came in – a thing they had never heard of before. I likewise insisted on another strange regulation, that the men and women should sit apart. A third was made the same day. It had been a custom, to have the galleries full of spectators while the Lord's Supper was administered. This I judged highly improper, and ordered none to be admitted but those who desired to communicate.

Wednesday, 2 May – [Mold, Flintshire] The sun was very hot and the wind very cold; but, as the place they had chose for me was exposed both to the sun and the wind, the one balanced the other. And, notwithstanding the Chester races, which had drawn the rich away, and the market-day, which detained many of the poor, we had a multitude of people, the serious part of whom soon influenced the rest; so that all but two or three remained uncovered, and kneeled down as soon as I began to pray.

Friday, 11 May – At Lancaster we were informed it was too late to cross the sands. However, we resolved to make the trial. We passed the seven-mile sand without difficulty, and reached Flookborough about sunset.

Saturday, 12 May – We came to Bootle, soon after eight, having crossed the Millom Sands without either guide or difficulty. We reached Whitehaven before night. But I have taken my leave of the sand-road. I believe it is ten measured miles shorter than the other; but there are four sands to pass, so far from each other that it is scarce possible to pass them all in a day – especially as you have all the way to do with a generation of liars, who detain all strangers as long as they can, either for their own gain or their neighbours'. I can advise no stranger to go this way: he may go round by Kendal and Keswick, often in less time, always with less expense, and far less trial of his patience.

Reflecting to-day on the case of a poor woman who had continual pain in her stomach, I could not but remark the inexcusable negligence of most physicians in cases of this nature. Whence came this woman's pain? From fretting for the death of her son. And what availed medicines while that fretting continued?

Monday, 4 June – I rode on to Newcastle. Certainly, if I did not believe there was another world, I should spend all my summers here, as I know no place in Great Britain comparable to it for pleasantness. But I seek another country, and therefore am content to be a wanderer upon earth.

Tuesday, 26 June – I preached abroad to twice the people we should have had at the house. What marvel the devil does not love field-preaching! Neither do I: I love a commodious room, a soft cushion, a handsome pulpit. But where is my zeal, if I do not trample all these underfoot in order to save one more soul?

Sunday, 15 July – [York] I began reading to the society an account of the late work of God at Everton; but I could not get through. At first there were only silent tears on every side, but it was not long before several were unable to refrain from weeping aloud; and quickly a stout young man dropped down and roared as in the agonies of death. I did not attempt to read any farther, but began wrestling with God in prayer. We continued herein till near nine o'clock. What a day of Jubilees was this!

Saturday, 21 July – Mr Grimshaw led us to a lone house on the side of an enormous mountain. The congregation stood and sat, row above row, in the sylvan theatre. I believe nothing on the post-diluvian earth can be more pleasant than the road from hence, between huge steep mountains, clothed with wood to the top, and washed at the bottom by a clear, winding stream.

Sunday, 5 August –[following an extended account of dramatic scenes at Everton] Between eight and nine I reached Everton, faint and weary enough. During the prayers, as also during the sermon and the administration of the sacrament, a few persons cried aloud; but it was not from sorrow or fear, but love and joy. The same I observed in several parts of the afternoon service. In the evening two or three persons fell to the ground, and were extremely convulsed; but none cried out.

Monday, 6 August – I have generally observed more or less of these outward symptoms to attend the beginning of a general work of God. So it was in New England, Scotland, Holland, Ireland, and many parts of England; but, after a time, they gradually decrease, and the work goes on more quietly and silently.

Tuesday, 7 August – After preaching at four (because of the harvest), I took horse and rode easily to London, thoroughly tired having rode in seven months above four-and-twenty hundred miles.

Wednesday, 8 August – Our Conference began, the time of which was employed in examining whether the spirit and lives of our preachers were suitable to their profession. Great was the unanimity and love that reigned among us; and if there were any who hoped or feared the contrary, they were happily disappointed.

Sunday, 9 September – [Norwich] I met the society at seven, and told them that they were the most ignorant, self-conceited, self-willed, fickle, untractable, disorderly, disjointed society that I knew in the three kingdoms. And God applied it to their hearts, so that many were profited; but I do not find that one was offended.

Friday, 21 September – [London] I read Mr Huygens's *Conjectures on the Planetary World*. I think he clearly proves that the moon is not habitable; that there are neither 'rivers nor mountains on her spotty globe'; that there is no sea, no water on her surface, nor any atmosphere. And hence he very rationally infers that 'neither are any of the secondary planets inhabited.' And who can prove that the primary are? I know the earth is. Of the rest I know nothing.

Monday, 15 October – [Bristol] I walked up to Knowle, to see the French prisoners. Above eleven hundred of them were confined in that little place without anything to lie on but a little dirty straw, or anything to cover them but a few foul, thin rags, either by day or night, so that they died like rotten sheep. I was much affected, and preached in the evening on Exodus 23:9 'Thou shalt not oppress a stranger; for ye know the heart of a stranger, seeing ye were strangers in the land of Egypt.' Eighteen pounds were contributed immediately, which were made up four-and-twenty the next day. With this we bought linen and woollen cloth, which were made up into shirts, waistcoats, and breeches. Some dozen of stockings were added; all which were carefully distributed where there was the greatest want.

Sunday, 4 November – [London] As I was applying those words, 'They neither marry, nor are given in marriage,' the power of God fell upon the congregation in a very uncommon manner. How seasonable! Oh how does God sweeten whatever cross we bear for his sake!

Saturday, 17 November – I spent an hour agreeably and profitably with Lady Gertrude, and Sir Charles Hotham. It is well a few of the rich and noble are called. Oh that God would increase their number! But I should rejoice (were it the will of God) if it were done by the ministry of others. If I might choose, I should still preach the gospel to the poor.

Friday, 23 November – The roads were so extremely slippery, it was with much difficulty we reached Bedford. We had a pretty large congregation, but the stench from the swine under the room was scarce supportable. Was ever a preaching-place over a hog-sty before? Surely they love the gospel who come to hear it in such a place.

Wednesday, 12 December – I spent part of the afternoon in the British Museum. There is a large library, a great number of curious manuscripts, many uncommon monuments of antiquity, and the whole collection of shells, butterflies, beetles, grasshoppers, etc, which the indefatigable Sir Hans Sloane, with such vast expense and labour, procured in a life of fourscore years.

1760

Tuesday, 5 February – I baptized a gentlewoman at the
Foundery, and the peace she immediately found was a fresh
proof that the outward sign, duly received, is always accompanied with the inward grace.

Thursday, 6 March – I talked largely with M. S., and Elizabeth
Longmore. The substance of what M. S. said was as follows: 'As
Mr Johnson was preaching one morning at five o'clock, in
Darlaston, my soul was so filled with the love of God that I had
much ado to help crying out. From this time I never committed
any known sin, nor ever lost the love of God.' Elizabeth
Longmore said: 'On Holy Thursday, 1756, my soul sunk into
nothing before God, and was filled with humble love. I loved
God and all mankind. Nor do I know that I ever committed any
wilful sin after I was justified.

'On Friday, January 25, as soon as Mr Fugill began to speak I
felt my soul was all love. I have never since found my heart
wander from God. He is never out of my thoughts: I search my
heart again and again; and I can find nothing but love there.'

I observe the spirit and experience of these two run exactly parallel. Constant communion with God the Father and the Son fills their hearts with humble love. Now this is what I always did, and do now, mean by perfection.

Wednesday, 12 March – [Leeds] I spent the greatest part of this day in examining them one by one. Concerning the far greatest part, it is plain (1) that they feel no inward sin, and to the best of their knowledge commit no outward sin; (2) that they see and love God every moment, and pray, rejoice, and give thanks evermore; (3) that they have constantly as clear a witness from God of sanctification as they have of justification. Now in this I do rejoice, and will rejoice, call it what you please.

Thursday, 20 March – [Liverpool] I had a good deal of conversation with John Newton. His case is very peculiar. Our Church requires that clergymen should be men of learning, and, to this end, have a university education. But how many have a university education, and yet no learning at all? Yet these men are ordained! Meantime, one of eminent learning, as well as unblamable behaviour, cannot be ordained *because he was not at the University!* What a mere farce is this!

Friday, 9 May – [Garragh, near Ballymena] A little rest was acceptable.

Saturday, 10 May – I preached to a well-behaved congregation, of various denominations: Churchmen, Papists, Presbyterians, Cameronians. One Seceder likewise ventured in; but the moment he heard 'Our Father, which art in heaven,' he ran away with all speed.

Tuesday, 27 May – [Castlebar] There was a remarkable trial here. A Swedish ship, being leaky, put into one of our harbours. The Irish, according to custom, ran to plunder her. A neighbouring gentleman hindered them, and, for so doing, demanded a fourth part of the cargo: and this, they said, the law allows! But where, meantime, is the law of God?

Thursday, 17 July – I met the classes at Limerick, and found a considerable decrease. And how can it be otherwise, when vice flows as a torrent, unless the children of God are all life, zeal, activity? In hopes of quickening them, I preached at seven in the old camp to more than twice the usual congregation; which the two next evenings was more numerous still, and equally attentive.

Sunday, 12 October – I visited the classes at Kingswood. Here there is no increase; and yet, where was there such a prospect till that weak man, John Cennick, confounded the poor people with strange doctrines? Oh what mischief may be done by one that means well!

On the three following days I spoke severally to the members of the society. As many of them increase in worldly goods, the great danger I apprehend now is their relapsing into the spirit of the world; and then their religion is but a dream.

Saturday, 25 October – King George was gathered to his fathers. When will England have a better Prince?

Monday, 17 November – [London] I sent the following letter:

TO THE EDITOR OF LLOYD'S EVENING POST

Sir,

The fundamental doctrine of the people called Methodists is, Whosoever will be saved, before all things it is necessary that he hold the true faith; the faith which works by love; which, by means of the love of God and our neighbour, produces both inward and outward holiness... He that thus believes is regenerate, or born of God; and he has the witness in himself (call it assurance, or what you please): the Spirit itself witnesses with his spirit that he is a child of God. 'From what Scripture' every one of these propositions 'is collected', any common Concordance will show.

Monday, 24 November – I visited the sick. How much better is it, to *carry* relief to the poor, than to *send* it! And that both for our own sake and theirs. For theirs, as it is so much more comfortable to them, and as we may then assist them in spirituals as well as temporals; and for our own, as it is far more apt to soften our heart, and to make us naturally care for each other.

Wednesday, 3 December – [Dover] Who would have expected to find here some of the best singers in England?

Friday, 12 December – Having as far as Hyde Park Corner to go, I took a coach for part of the way, ordering the man to stop anywhere at the end of Piccadilly next the Haymarket. He stopped exactly at the door of one of our friends, whose mother, above ninety years old, had long desired to see me, though I knew it not. She was exceedingly comforted, and could not tell how to praise God enough for giving her the desire of her soul.

1761

Thursday, 19 March – [Burslem] I preached at half-hour past five, in an open place on the top of the hill, to a large and attentive congregation, though it rained almost all the time and the air was extremely cold. The next morning (being Good Friday) I did not preach till eight. But even then, as well as in the evening, the cold considerably lessened the congregation. Such is human wisdom! So small are the things which divert mankind from what might be the means of their eternal salvation!

Wednesday, 22 April – About noon I preached at Branthwaite, and in the evening at Lorton. Who would imagine that Deism should find its way into the heart of these enormous mountains?

Saturday, 25 April – As the people at Whitehaven are usually full of zeal, right or wrong, I this evening showed them the nature of Christian zeal. Perhaps some of them may now distinguish the flame of love from a fire kindled in hell.

Monday, 27 April – I preached at eight in the market-place at Wigton. The congregation, when I began, consisted of one woman, two boys, and three or four little girls, but in a quarter of an hour we had most of the town.

Monday, 11 May – [Edinburgh] The situation of the city, on a hill shelving down on both sides, with the stately castle upon a craggy rock on the west, is inexpressibly fine. And the main street, so broad and finely paved, with the lofty houses on either hand (many of them seven or eight stories high), is far beyond any in Great Britain. But how can it be suffered that all manner of filth should still be thrown even into this street continually? How long shall the capital city of Scotland, yea, and the chief street of it, stink worse than a common sewer?

Monday, 26 May – [South Shields] Why is there not here (as in every parish in England) a particular minister who takes care of all their souls? There is one here who takes *charge* of all their souls; what *care* of them he takes is another question. It may be he neither knows nor cares whether they are going to heaven or hell. Does he ask man, woman, or child any question about it from one Christmas to the next? Oh, what account will such a pastor give to the Great Shepherd in that day?

Tuesday, 9 June – [Weardale] I met the society, and came just in time to prevent their all turning Dissenters, which they were on the point of doing, being quite disgusted at the curate, whose life was no better than his doctrine.

Sunday, 12 July – [Haworth] The church would not near contain the people who came from all sides; however, Mr Grimshaw had provided for this by fixing a scaffold on the outside of one of the windows, through which I went after prayers, and the people likewise all went out into the churchyard. The afternoon congregation was larger still. What has God wrought in the midst of those rough mountains!

Sunday, 19 July – [Birstall] Many were surprised when I told them, 'The very design of a lovefeast is free and familiar conversation, in which every man, yea, and woman, has liberty to speak whatever may be to the glory of God.' Several then did speak, and not in vain; the flame ran from heart to heart, especially while one was declaring, with all simplicity, the manner wherein God, during the morning sermon, had set her soul at full liberty.

Monday, 20 July – I came to a full explanation with that good man Mr Venn. Lord, if I must dispute, let it be with the children of the devil! Let me be at peace with thy children!

Friday, 24 July – [Kippax] Mr Venn came a little after we were gone into the church. Mr Romaine read prayers. I preached on 'Christ crucified, to the Jews a stumbling-block, and to the Greeks foolishness.' Oh why should they who agree in this great point fall out about smaller things?

Thursday, 13 September – [Boston] The church is indeed a fine building. It is larger, loftier, nay, and rather more lightsome than even St Peter's at Norwich, and the steeple is, I suppose, the highest tower in England, nor less remarkable for the architecture than the height.

Tuesday, 13 October – I preached at Newgate, at Kingswood in the afternoon, and in the evening at North Common. Here a people are sprung up, as it were, out of the earth, most of them employed in the neighbouring brass-works. We took a view of these the next day, and I learned here, the propriety of that expression, Revelation 1:15, 'His feet were as fine brass, burning in a furnace.' The brightness of this cannot easily be conceived; I have seen nothing like it but clear white lightning.

Wednesday, 21 October – I was desired by the condemned prisoners to give them one sermon more. And on Thursday Patrick Ward, who was to die on that day, sent to request I would administer the sacrament to him. He was one-and-twenty years of age, and had scarce ever had a serious thought till he shot the man who went to take away his gun.

Thursday, 26 November – I was desired to read part of Bishop Pontoppidan's *Natural History of Norway*. I soon found he was a man of sense, yet credulous to an extreme; and therefore I was the less surprised when I came to his craken and sea-serpent.

1762

'Messiah, Prince of Peace,
Where men each other tear,
Where war is learned, they must confess,
Thy kingdom is not there;
Who prompted by thy foe
Delight in human blood,
Apollyon is their King, we know,
And Satan is their god.'
                Charles Wesley, *Scripture Hymns* 1762

Sunday, 14 February – I buried the remains of Thomas Salmon, a good and useful man. What was peculiar in his experience was, he did not know when he was justified; but he did know when he was renewed in love, that work being wrought in a most distinct manner. After this he continued about a year in constant love, joy, and peace; then, after an illness of a few days, he cheerfully went to God.

Wednesday, 21 April – Where to preach in Belfast I did not know. It was too wet to preach abroad, and a dancing-master was busily employed in the upper part of the market-house, till at twelve the sovereign put him out by holding his court there. While he was above, I began below to a very serious and attentive audience. But they were all poor; the rich of Belfast 'cared for none of these things.'

Friday, 30 April – We came in the evening to a lone house called Carrickbeg. It lay in the midst of horrid mountains, and had no very promising appearance. However, it afforded corn for our horses and potatoes for ourselves. So we made a hearty supper, called in as many as pleased of the family to prayers, and slept in peace.

Monday, 3 May – In the evening a company of players began acting in the upper part of the market-house just as we began singing in the lower. On Tuesday evening the lower part too was occupied by buyers and sellers of oatmeal, but as soon as I began the people quitted their sacks and listened to business of greater importance.

Monday, 7 June – [Newmarket] I met a large number of children, just as much acquainted with God, and with the things of God, as 'a wild ass's colt.' And yet who can believe that these pretty little creatures have 'the wrath of God abiding on them?'

Numberless crowds ran together about this time to see the execution of a poor deserter. And I believe some of them retained serious impressions for near four-and-twenty hours! But it was not so with the soldiers, although they walked one by one, close to the bleeding, mangled carcase, most of them were as merry within six hours as if they had only seen a puppet-show.

Sunday, 13 June – Being informed I had shot over the heads of the soldiers, who did not 'understand anything but hell and damnation,' I took my leave of them this evening by strongly applying the story of Dives and Lazarus. They seemed to understand this.

Monday, 12 July – I went to Dunmore Cave, three or four miles from Kilkenny. On one side of the cave is a narrow passage which goes under the rock two or three hundred yards; on the other a hollow, which no one has ever been able to find an end of. I suppose this hole too, as well as many others, was formed by the waters of the deluge retreating into the great abyss, with which probably it communicates.

Saturday, 17 July – I went on to poor dead Portarlington. And no wonder it should be so while the preachers coop themselves up in a room with twenty or thirty hearers. I went straight to the market-place and cried aloud, 'Harken! Behold a sower went forth to sow.' God made his word quick and powerful, and sharp as a two-edged sword.

Wednesday, 28 July – I received further accounts from Limerick; one ran thus:

20 July 1762. There is a glorious work going on at Limerick. Twelve or fourteen have a clear sense of being renewed; several have been justified this week; and on Sunday night, there was such a cry as I scarce ever heard before, such confession of sins, such pleading with the Lord, and such a spirit of prayer, as if the Lord himself had been visibly present among us. Some received remission of sins, and several were just brought to the birth. All were in floods of tears; they trembled, they cried, they prayed, they roared aloud, all of them lying on the ground. I began to sing, yet they could not rise, but sang as they lay along. Some of them stayed in the house all night; and, blessed be our Lord, they all hitherto walk worthy of their calling.

Friday, 20 August – [London] As I expected, the sower of tares had not been idle during my five months' absence; but, I believe great part of his work was undone in one hour, when we met at West Street.

Saturday, 28 August – [Exeter] When I began the service there the congregation (beside ourselves) were two women and one man. Before I had done the room was about half full. This comes of omitting field-preaching.

Sunday, 29 August – At the cathedral we had a useful sermon, and the whole service was performed with great seriousness and decency. Such an organ I never saw or heard before, and the music of 'Glory be to God in the highest,' I think, exceeded the *Messiah* itself. I was well pleased to partake of the Lord's Supper with my old opponent, Bishop Lavington. Oh, may we sit down together in the kingdom of our Father!

Tuesday, 14 September – I preached in the evening, near the quay at St Ives. Two or three pretty butterflies came, and looked, and smiled, and went away; but all the rest of the numerous congregation behaved with the utmost seriousness.

Wednesday, 15 September – We had our Quarterly meeting. The more I converse with the believers in Cornwall, the more I am convinced that they have sustained great loss for want of hearing the doctrine of Christian Perfection clearly and strongly enforced.

Thursday, 28 October – One who had adorned the gospel in life and in death having desired that I should preach her funeral sermon, I went with a few friends to the house and sang before the body to the room. I did this the rather to show my approbation of that solemn custom and to encourage others to follow it.

Many years ago my brother frequently said: 'Your day of Pentecost is not fully come, but I doubt not it will, and you will then hear of persons sanctified as frequently as you do now of persons justified.' Any unprejudiced reader may observe that it was now fully come.

Monday, 1 November – [Canterbury] Here I seriously reflected on some late occurrences, and, after weighing the matter thoroughly, wrote as follows [to Thomas Maxfield]:

Without any preface or ceremony, which is needless between you and me, I will simply and plainly tell what I dislike in your doctrine, spirit, or outward behaviour...

But what I most of all dislike is, your littleness of love to your brethren; your want of meekness, gentleness, longsuffering; your impatience of contradiction; your counting every man your enemy that reproves or admonishes you in love, your bigotry and narrowness of spirit...

As to your public meetings, I like the praying fervently and largely for all the blessings of God; and I know much good has been done hereby, and hope much more will be done.

But I dislike several things therein: (1) the singing, or speaking, or praying, of several at once; (2) the praying to the Son of God only, or more than to the Father; (3) the using improper expressions in prayer; sometimes too pompous and magnificent, extolling yourselves rather than God, and telling him what you are, not what you want; (4) using poor, flat, bald hymns; (5) the never kneeling at prayer; (6) your using postures or gestures highly indecent; (7) your screaming, even so as to make the words unintelligible...

    Your affectionate brother,
    John Wesley.

Wednesday, 8 December – [London] I observed a few of our brethren were diligently propagating that principle that none can teach those who are renewed in love unless he be in the state himself. I saw the tendency of this, but I saw that violent remedies would not avail.

Friday, 31 December – I now stood and looked back on the past year; a year of uncommon trials and uncommon blessings. Abundance have been convinced of sin; very many have found peace with God; and in London only, I believe, full two hundred have been brought into glorious liberty. And yet I have had more care and trouble in six months than in several years preceding. What the end will be, I know not; but it is enough that God knoweth.

1763

'Outcasts of men, to you I call,
  Harlots, and publicans, and thieves!
He spreads his arms t'embrace you all
  Sinners alone his grace receives:
No need of him the righteous have,
He came the lost to seek and save.'
    Charles Wesley, *Hymns and Sacred Poems*, 1739
    (probably written at his conversion the previous
    year)

Friday, 7 January – I desired George Bell to meet me with one or two others. We took much pains to convince him of his mistakes, particularly that which he had lately adopted – that the end of the world was to be on February 28.

Monday, 21 February – Observing the terror occasioned by that wonderful prophecy to spread far and wide, I endeavoured to draw some good therefrom by strongly exhorting the congregation at Wapping to 'seek the Lord while he might be found.'

Monday, 28 February – Preaching in the evening at Spitalfields on 'Prepare to meet thy God,' I largely showed the utter absurdity of the supposition that the world was to end that night. But notwithstanding all I could say, many were afraid to go to bed, and some wandered about in the fields, being persuaded that at least London would be swallowed up by an earthquake. I went to bed at my usual time, and was fast asleep about ten o'clock.

Sunday, 29 May – I preached at seven in the High School yard at Edinburgh. It being the time of the General Assembly, which drew together, not the ministers only, but abundance of the nobility and gentry, many of both sorts were present; but abundantly more at five in the afternoon. I spoke as plain as ever I did in my life; but I never knew any in Scotland offended at plain dealing.

Tuesday, 7 June – [Barnard Castle] There is something remarkable in the manner wherein God revived his work in these parts. A few months ago the generality of people in this circuit were exceeding lifeless. Samuel Meggot, perceiving this, advised the society to observe every Friday with fasting and prayer. The very first Friday they met together God broke in upon them in a wonderful manner; and his work has been increasing among them ever since. Is not the neglect of fasting one general occasion of deadness among Christians?

Saturday, 20 August – [After visiting Howell Harris at Trevecca] We rode through one of the pleasantest countries in the world. When we came to Trecastle we had rode fifty miles in Monmouthshire and Brecknockshire; and I will be bold to say all England does not afford such a line of fifty miles' length, for fields, meadows, woods, brooks, and gently rising mountains, fruitful to the very top.

Thursday, 25 August – [Haverfordwest] I was more convinced than ever that the preaching like an apostle, without joining together those that are awakened and training them up in the ways of God, is only begetting children for the murderer. How much preaching has there been for these twenty years all over Pembrokeshire! But no regular societies, no discipline, no order or connexion; and nine in ten of the once-awakened are now faster asleep than ever.

Sunday, 28 August – I preached once more in Wenvoe Church; but it was hard work. Mr Hodges read the prayers (not as he did once, with such fervour and solemnity as struck almost every hearer) but like one reading an old song, in a cold, dry, careless manner; and there was no singing at all.

Thence I rode to Cardiff, and found the society in as ruinous a condition as the Castle. The same poison of Mysticism has wellnigh extinguished the last spark of life here also.

Sunday, 4 September – [Bristol] I preached on the quay, where multitudes attended who would not have come to the other end of the city. In the afternoon I preached near the new Square. I find no other way to reach the outcasts of men.

Monday, 19 September – I gave our brethren a solemn caution not to 'love the world, neither the things of the world.' This will be their grand danger; as they are industrious and frugal, they must needs increase in goods. In London, Bristol, and most other trading towns, those who are in business have increased in substance sevenfold, some of them twenty, yea, an hundredfold. What need, then, have these of the strongest warnings, lest they be entangled therein, and perish!

Saturday, 1 October – I returned to London and found our house in ruins, great part of it being taken down, in order to a thorough repair. But as much remained as I wanted – six foot square suffices me by day or by night.

Friday, 16 November – Here I stood and looked back. Before Thomas Walsh left England God began that great work which has continued ever since without any considerable intermission. During the whole time many have been convinced of sin, many justified, and many backsliders healed. But the peculiar work of this season has been what St Paul calls 'perfecting of the saints.' Many persons in various parts, both of England and Ireland, have experienced so deep and universal a change as it had not before entered into their hearts to conceive. After a deep conviction of inbred sin, they have been so filled with faith and love (and generally in a moment) that sin vanished, and they found from that time no pride, anger, desire, or unbelief.

Thursday, 22 December – I spent a little time in a visit to Mr M–; twenty years ago a zealous and useful magistrate, now a picture of human nature in disgrace – feeble in body and mind, slow of speech and of understanding. Lord, let me not live to be useless!

1764

'Good Friday, 20 April, 1764 – I have made no reformation;
I have lived totally useless, more sensual in thought, and
more addicted to wine and meat...

April 21 – My indolence, since my last reception of the
sacrament has sunk into grosser sluggishness. A strange
kind of oblivion has overcome me, so that I know not what
has become of the last year. This is not the life to which
heaven is promised.'

Samuel Johnson, from *Prayers and Meditations*

Monday, 16 January – [High Wycombe] My face and gums were
so swelled I could hardly speak. After I took horse they grew
worse and worse, till it began to rain. I was then persuaded to put
on an oil-case hood, which kept rubbing continually on my cheek
till both pain and swelling were gone.

Between twelve and one we crossed Ensham Ferry. The water
was like a sea on both sides. I asked the ferryman, 'Can we ride
the causeway?' He said, 'Yes, sir; if you keep in the middle.' But
this was the difficulty, as the whole causeway was covered with
water to a considerable depth and this ran over the causeway
with the swiftness and violence of a sluice. Once my mare lost
both her fore feet, but she gave a spring, and recovered the
causeway; otherwise we must have taken a swim. However,
after one or two plunges more, we got through, and came safe to
Witney.

The congregation in the evening was both large and deeply
attentive.

Thursday, 19 January – [Henley] I found a wild, staring congregation, many of them void both of common sense and
common decency.

Monday, 23 January – I rode to Sundon, and preached to a very quiet and very stupid people. After all our preaching here, even those who have constantly attended no more understand us than if we had preached in Greek.

Thursday, 26 January – I tried another way to reach them. I preached on 'Where their worm dieth not, and the fire is not quenched;' and set before them the terrors of the Lord, in the strongest manner I was able. It seemed to be the very thing they wanted.

Thursday, 2 February – I preached again in the Foundery, which had been repairing for several weeks. It is not only firm and safe (whereas before the main timbers were quite decayed) but clean and decent, and capable of receiving several hundreds more.

Thursday, 16 February – I once more took a serious walk through the tombs in Westminster Abbey. What heaps of unmeaning stone and marble! But there was one tomb which showed common sense: that beautiful figure of Mr Nightingale endeavouring to screen his lovely wife from Death.

Wednesday, 29 February – I heard *Judith*, an oratorio, performed at the Lock. Some parts of it were exceeding fine; but there are two things in all modern pieces of music which I could never reconcile to common sense. One is singing the same words ten times over; the other, singing different words by different persons, at one and the same time. And this in the most solemn addresses to God; this can never be defended by all the musicians in Europe, till reason is quite out of date.

Wednesday, 21 March – We stopped at a little village. We easily perceived by the marks he had left, that the man of the house had been beating his wife. I took occasion from thence to speak strongly to her concerning the hand of God, and his design in all afflictions. She appeared to be not only thankful, but deeply affected.

We had an exceeding large congregation at Birmingham, in what was formerly the playhouse. Happy would it be if the playhouses in the kingdom were converted to so good a use.

Monday, 26 March – [Ashby-de-la-Zouch] The house and yard contained the people tolerably well. I saw but one trifler among all, which, I understood, was an attorney. Poor man! If men live what I preach, the hope of his gain is lost.

Saturday, 31 March – [Rotherham] An odd circumstance occurred during the morning preaching. It was well only serious persons were present. An ass walked gravely in at the gate, came up to the door, lifted up his head and stood stock-still, in a posture of deep attention. Might not 'the dumb beast reprove' many who have far less decency, and not much more understanding?

Friday, 20 April (being *Good Friday*) – We had a parting blessing at five. I then rode to Robin Hood's Bay, and about two preached in the little square. At six I preached in the new house at Whitby, ill containing the congregation. Here God does still make bare his arm, and sinners are continually converted to him.

Saturday, 19 May – We rode by a great house I had frequently heard of. The front is truly noble. In the house I saw nothing remarkable but what was remarkably bad: such pictures as an honest heathen would be ashamed to receive under his roof, unless he designed his wife and daughters should be common prostitutes. And this is the high fashion!

Wednesday, 23 May – I rode over the sands to Holy Island, once the famous seat of a bishop; now the residence of a few poor families, who live chiefly by fishing. At one side of the town are the ruins of a cathedral, with an adjoining monastery. I preached to almost all the inhabitants of the island, and distributed some little books among them, for which they were exceeding thankful.

Thursday, 31 May – [Dundee] There is seldom fear of wanting a congregation in Scotland. But the misfortune is, they know everything; so they learn nothing.

Monday, 11 June – After Edinburgh, Glasgow, and Aberdeen, I think Inverness is the largest town I have seen in Scotland. The main streets are broad and straight; the houses mostly old, but not very bad nor very good. It stands in a pleasant and fruitful country, and has all things needful for life and godliness. The people in general speak remarkably good English.

Oh what a difference is there between South and North Britain! Every one here at least loves to hear the word of God; and none takes it into his head to speak an uncivil word to any for endeavouring to save their souls.

Tuesday, 12 June – Among all the sins they have imported from England, the Scots have not yet learned to scoff at sacred things.

Monday, 2 July – [Leeds] I gave a fair hearing to two of our brethren who had proved bankrupts. Such we immediately exclude from our society, unless it plainly appears not to be their own fault.

Friday, 13 July – At ten I began to preach at Wigan, proverbially famous for all manner of wickedness. We expected some disturbance; but there was none at all.

Monday, 16 July – [Liverpool] I preached on the 'one thing needful', and the rich behaved as seriously as the poor. Only one young gentlewoman laughed much. Poor thing! Doubtless she thought, 'I laugh prettily.'

Monday, 6 August – [Bristol] Our Conference began. The great point I now laboured for was a good understanding with all of the clergy who are heartily engaged in propagating vital religion.

Sunday, 4 November – [London] I proposed to the leaders the assisting the Society for the Reformation of Manners with regard to their heavy debt. One of them asked, 'Ought we not to pay our own debt first?' After some consultations, it was agreed to attempt it. The debt of the society in London, occasioned chiefly by repairing the Foundery and chapels, and by building at Wapping and Snowsfields, was about nine hundred pounds.

Monday, 5 November – My scraps of time this week I employed in setting down my thoughts upon a single life, which indeed, are the same they have been these thirty years; and the same they must be, unless I give up my Bible.

Monday, 31 December – I thought it would be worth while to make an odd experiment. Remembering how surprisingly fond of music the lion at Edinburgh was, I went to the Tower with one who plays on the German flute. He began playing near four or five lions; only one of these rose up, came to the front of his den, and seemed to be all attention. Meantime, a tiger leaped over the lion's back, turned and ran under his belly, leaped over him again, and so to and fro incessantly.

1765

'The believer has many enemies opposing him in his way heavenwards; but in Christ he has strength sufficient to conquer them all. His worst enemy, that gives him most uneasiness, is indwelling sin, which is never at rest, like the troubled sea, always casting up some of its filthy motions and corruptions; so that when he is at prayer, it is ever trying to amuse and distract his mind with a thousand vain and idle thoughts... Over this enemy there is no victory but by faith.'

William Romaine, *A treatise upon the Life of Faith*

Tuesday, 1 January – I wrote an answer to a warm letter, in *The London Magazine*, the author whereof is much displeased that I presume to doubt of the modern astronomy. I cannot help it. Nay, the more I consider, the more my doubts increase.

Sunday, 30 January – I looked over Mr Romaine's strange book on the *Life of Faith*. I thought nothing could ever exceed Mr Ingham's; but really this does. I employed all my leisure hours this week in revising my letters and papers. Abundance of them I committed to the flames. Perhaps some of the rest may see the light when I am gone.

Wednesday, 13 February – I heard *Ruth*, an oratorio, at Mr Madan's chapel. The sense was admirable and much of the poetry not contemptible. This, joined with exquisite music, might possibly make an impression even upon rich and honourable sinners.

Sunday, 10 March – [London] I made a collection for the poor weavers who are out of employment. It amounted to about forty pounds.

Wednesday, 1 May – The wind was quite fair; so, as soon as the tide served, I went on board [for Ireland]. It seemed strange to cross the sea in an open boat, especially when the waves ran high. I was a little sick, till I fell asleep. In five hours and a half we reached Donaghadee; but my mare could not land till five hours after.

Sunday, 12 May – [Londonderry] About eleven Mr Knox went with me to church, and led me to a pew where I was placed next the mayor. What is this? What have I to do with honour? Lord, let me always *fear*, not *desire* it.

Saturday, 25 May – Ever since I came hither I have been amazed at the honesty which runs through this city. None scruples to leave his house open all day, and the door only on the latch at night. Such a thing as theft is scarce heard of at Derry; no one has the least suspicion of it. No wonder, therefore, that the inhabitants never suspect themselves to be sinners.

Saturday, 13 July – I read Sir Richard Cox's *History of Ireland*. I suppose it is accounted as authentic as any that is extant. But surely never was there the like in the habitable world! Such a series of robberies, murders, and burning of houses, towns, and countries did I never hear or read of before. I do not wonder Ireland is thinly inhabited, but that it has any inhabitants at all.

Thursday, 18 July – [Dublin] I began expounding the deepest part of the Holy Scripture, the first Epistle of St John, by which, above all other, even inspired writings, I advise every young preacher to form his style. Here are sublimity and simplicity together, the strongest sense and the plainest language!

Thursday, 8 August – [Newcastle] I scarce ever saw the people here so much alive to God. I was ready to say, 'It is good for me to be here'; but I must not build tabernacles. I am to be a wanderer on earth, and desire no rest till my spirit returns to God.

Wednesday, 11 September – [Cornwall] Perceiving my voice begin to fail, I resolved to preach, for a while, but twice a day.

Monday, 28 October – [London] I breakfasted with Mr Whitefield, who seemed to be an old, old, man, being fairly worn out in his Master's service, though he has hardly seen fifty years. And yet it pleases God that I, who am now in my sixty-third year, find no disorder, no weakness, no decay, only that I have fewer teeth and more grey hairs.

Wednesday, 18 December – Riding through the Borough, all my mare's feet flew up, and she fell with my leg under her. A gentleman lifted me up, and helped me into his shop. I was exceeding sick, but was presently relieved by a little hartshorn and water. I went on to Shoreham; where, by applying treacle twice a day, all the soreness was removed, and I recovered some strength, so as to be able to walk a little on plain ground.

Thursday, 26 December – I should have been glad of a few days' rest, but it could not be at this busy season. However, being electrified morning and evening, my lameness mended, though but slowly.

1766

'He sent his two Servants, Whitefield and Westley: were
    they Prophets,
Or were they Idiots or Madmen? Shew us Miracles!
Can you have greater Miracles than these? Men who devote
Their life's whole comfort to intire scorn and injury and
    death?
Awake, thou sleeper on the Rock of Eternity! Albion
    awake!
The trumpet of Judgement hath twice sounded...'
    William Blake: from 'Milton', 1804-8

Friday, 3 January – Mr B called upon me, now calm and in his
right mind. God has repressed his furious, bitter zeal by means
of Mr Whitefield. He (Mr Whitefield) made the first breach
among the Methodists; oh that God may empower him to heal it!

Friday, 31 January – Mr Whitefield called upon me. He breathes
nothing but peace and love. Bigotry cannot stand before him,
but hides its head wherever he comes.

Wednesday, 12 March – I rode over to Kingswood, and, having
told my whole mind to the masters and servants, spoke to the
children in a far stronger manner than ever I did before. I will kill
or cure: I will have one or the other – a Christian school, or none
at all.

Tuesday, 15 April – In riding over the dreary mountains of the
High Peak we met with several storms; but we were no worse
when we came to Rotherham, where I preached in the evening.

The spirit of the congregation was able to liven the dullest preacher. Indeed it was good to be here.

Wednesday, 21 May – [Alnwick] We spent an hour in the Castle and the gardens, which the Duke is enlarging and improving daily, and turning into a little paradise. What a pity that he must leave all these, and die like a common man!

Monday, 26 May – [Edinburgh] I spent some hours at the meeting of the National Assembly [of the Church of Scotland]. I was extremely shocked at the behaviour of many of the members. Had any preacher behaved so at our Conference he would have had no more place among us.

Thursday, 5 June – [Dundee] The sum of what I spoke was this:

I love plain dealing. Do not you? I will use it now. Bear with me.

I am a member of the Church of England: but I love good men of every Church.

My ground is the Bible. Yea, I am a Bible-bigot. I follow it in all things, both great and small.

Therefore, 1. I always use a short private prayer when I attend the public service of God. Do not you? Why do you not? Is not this according to the Bible?

2. I stand whenever I sing the praise of God in public. Does not the Bible give you plain precendents for this?

3. I always kneel before the Lord my Maker when I pray in public.

4. I generally in public use the Lord's Prayer, because Christ has taught me, when I pray, to say –

I advise every preacher connected with me, whether in England or Scotland, herein to tread in my steps.

Monday, 16 June – [Edinburgh] I took a view of one of the greatest natural curiosities in the kingdom – what is called Arthur's Seat: a small, rocky eminence, six or seven yards across, on the top of an exceeding high mountain, not far from Edinburgh. The prospect from the top of the Castle is large, but it is nothing in comparison of this.

Monday, 23 June – I met with Mr Knox's *History of the Church of Scotland*; and could any man wonder if the members of it were fierce, sour, and bitter of spirit? For what a pattern have they before them! It is said, 'The work to be done needed such a spirit.' Not so; the work of God does not, cannot need the work of the devil to forward it. God did use, at the time of the Reformation, some sour, overbearing, passionate men, yet he did not use them *because* they were such, but *notwithstanding* they were so. And there is no doubt he would have used them much more had they been of a humbler and milder spirit.

Thursday, 3 July – We rode through a pleasant vale to Wolsingham, where I began singing near the middle of the town. A few soon gathered together, and their number increased all the time I was preaching.

Wednesday, 20 August – [London] It was the earnest request of –, whose heart God has turned again, that I came hither so suddenly: and if no other good result from it but our firm union with Mr Whitefield, it is an abundant recompense for my labour. My brother and I conferred with him every day; and, let the honourable men do what they please, we resolved, by the grace of God, to go on, hand in hand, through honour and dishonour.

Tuesday, 25 August – Many were not a little surprised at seeing me in the Countess of Huntingdon's chapel. The congregation was not only large, but serious, and I fully delivered my own soul. So I am in no concern whether I preach there again or no.

Monday, 15 September – [Port Isaac] Mr Buckingham met me, who, for fear of offending the Bishop, broke off all commerce with the Methodists. He had no sooner done this than the Bishop rewarded him by turning him out of his curacy.

Monday, 6 October – Several evenings this week I preached at Bristol on the Education of Children. Some answered all by that poor, lame miserable shift, 'Oh, he has no children of his own!' But many, of a nobler spirit, owned the truth, and pleaded guilty before God.

Friday, 10 October – [Cheltenham] I examined the little society, and found the greater part of them quite free from the bigotry which is common among Churchmen and still more among Dissenters.

Sunday, 26 October – How pleasing would it be to ply between Bristol and London, and preach always to such congregations as these! But what account then should I give of my stewardship when I can 'be no longer steward'?

Wednesday, 5 November – [Sevenoaks] In the little journeys which I have lately taken, I have thought much on the huge encomiums which have been for many ages bestowed on a *country life*. But what a flat contradiction is this to universal experience! There is not a less happy body of men in all England than the country farmers, In general, their life is supremely dull; and it is usually unhappy too.

1767

Tuesday, 20 January – I buried the remains of Ann Wheeler, who, while she was hearing the preaching in Moorfields, four or five and twenty years ago, was struck in the forehead with a stone, being then big with child. The daughter with whom she then went retains the mark of the stone in her forehead to this day.

Saturday, 4 April – [Newry] When I began I had only four hearers. A good number assembled before I had done, only none of the gentry; they were hindered by a business of more importance – dressing for the assembly!

Saturday, 9 May – [Ireland] I rode to Ennis, but found the preaching had been discontinued, and the society was vanished away. So having no business there, I left it in the morning, preached at Clara about eight, and in the evening at Limerick. The continued rain kept me from preaching abroad this week; and I was scandalized at the smallness of the congregation in the house. I am afraid my glorying touching many of these societies is at an end.

Friday, 12 June – [Kilkenny] At noon, I expected to have seen the largest company of all; but I was mistaken: the ladies could not rise so soon; at least, they could not huddle on their clothes fit to be seen.

Monday, 15 June – [Aughrim] I had no place to retire to, and so was obliged to be in genteel company for two or three hours together. Oh what a dull thing is life without religion! I do not wonder that time hangs heavy upon the hands of all who know not God, unless they are perpetually drunk with noise and hurry of one kind or another.

Friday, 17 July – We lost our way in setting out of the town. It rained most of the day; however, this was far better than sultry heat. In the evening we returned to Dublin.

In my scraps of time this week I read over that wonderful poem, *Fingal.* If it is genuine, if it is really extant in the Erse language, it is an amazing proof of a genuis in those barbarous times; little inferior to Homer or Virgil!

Sunday, 2 August – [Glasgow] I was sorry to find both the society and the congregations smaller than when I was here last. I impute this chiefly to the manner of preaching which has been generally used. The people have been told, frequently and strongly, of their coldness, deadness, heaviness, and littleness of faith, but very rarely of anything that would move thankfulness. Hereby many were driven away, and those that remained were kept cold and dead.

Saturday, 8 August – [Newcastle] At the request of Mr Whitaker, of New England, I made a collection for the Indian schools in America. A large sum of money is now collected; but will money convert heathens? Find preachers of David Brainerd's spirit, and nothing can stand before them; but, without this, what will gold or silver do? They have indeed sent thousands to hell; but never yet brought a soul to heaven.

Tuesday, 25 August – I read Mr Crantz's *Account of the Mission into Greenland*. What a pity that so affecting an account should be disgraced with those vile, doggerel verses; just calculated to make the whole performance stink in the nostrils of all sensible men!

Monday, 23 November – [Canterbury] In the afternoon I rode to Dover, but the gentleman I was to lodge with was gone a long journey. He went to bed well, but was dead in the morning. Such a vapour is life!

1768

Monday, 4 January – At my leisure hours this week, I read Dr Priestley's ingenious book on Electricity. He seems to have accurately collected and well digested all that is known on that curious subject.

Monday, 11 January – This week I spent my scraps of time in reading Mr Woodrow's *History of the Sufferings of the Church of Scotland*. Oh what a blessed governor was that *good-natured* man, so called, King Charles the Second! Bloody Queen Mary was a lamb, a mere dove, in comparison of him!

Tuesday, 22 March – I read over a small book, *Poems*, by Miss Whateley, a farmer's daughter. She had little advantage from education, but an astonishing genius. Some of her elegies I think quite equal to Mr Gray's. If she had proper helps for a few years I question whether she would not have excelled any female poet that has ever yet appeared in England.

Thursday, 24 March – I rode to Newcastle-under-Lyme, one of the prettiest towns in England. Many here already know themselves: not a few know Christ.

Tuesday, 5 April – I preached at Warrington; I am afraid, not to the taste of some of my hearers, as my subject led me to speak strongly and explicitly on the Godhead of Christ. But that I cannot help, for on this I *must* insist as the foundation of all our hope.

Sunday, 1 May – [Aberdeen] I preached in the Castle-gate, on the paved stones. A large number of people were all attention; but there were many rude, stupid creatures round about them, who knew as little of reason as of religion; I never saw such brutes in Scotland before. One of them threw a potato.

Friday, 20 May – I went on in reading that fine book, Bishop Butler's *Analogy*. But I doubt it is too hard for most of those for whom it is chiefly intended. *Freethinkers*, so called, are seldom *close thinkers*.

Wednesday, 25 May – [Sunderland] The English in general, and indeed most of the men of learning in Europe, have given up all accounts of witches and apparitions, as mere old wives' fables. I am sorry for it; and I willingly take this opportunity of entering my solemn protest against this violent compliment which so many that believe the Bible pay to those who do not believe it. [An account of ghosts follows.]

Sunday, 7 August – [Pembroke] I took a good deal of pains to compose the little misunderstandings which have much obstructed the work of God, and the next morning left the people full of good desires, and in tolerable good humour with each other.

Tuesday, 9 August – [Neath] I was greatly disgusted at the manner of singing: (1) twelve or fourteen persons kept it to themselves, and quite shut out the congregation; (2) these repeated the same words, contrary to all sense and reason, six or eight or ten times over; (3) according to the shocking custom of modern music, different persons sung different words at one and the same moment; an intolerable insult on common sense, and utterly incompatible with any devotion.

Sunday, 14 August – [Bristol] Hearing my wife was dangerously ill, I took chaise immediately, and reached the Foundery before one in the morning. Finding that fever was turned, and the danger over, about two I set out again, and in the afternoon came (not at all tired) to Bristol.

Wednesday, 31 August – [St Ives] I met the children, a work which will exercise the talents of the most able preachers in England.

Thursday, 29 September – [Frome] The people here seem more alive than most; and this is the more strange because in this town there is such a mixture of all opinions – Anabaptists, Quakers, Presbyterians, Arians, Antinomians, Moravians, and what not. If any hold to the truth in the midst of all these, surely the power must be of God.

Friday, 14 October – I dined with Dr Wrangel, one of the King of Sweden's chaplains, who has spent several years in Pennsylvania. His heart seemed to be greatly united to the American Christians, and he strongly pleaded for our sending some of our preachers to help them.

Saturday, 22 October – I was much surprised in reading on 'Essay on Music' to find that the music of the ancients was as simple as that of the Methodists; that their music wholly consisted of melody, or the arrangement of single notes; that what is now call harmony, singing in parts, the whole of counterpoint and fugues, is quite novel.

Thursday, 1 December – I made an odd observation here, which I recommend to all our preachers. The people of Canterbury have been so often reproved for being dead and cold, that it has utterly discouraged them. How delicate a thing is it to reprove! To do it well requires more than human wisdom.

Friday, 2 December – Those who are called Mr Whitefield's society at Chatham offered me the use of their preaching-house. In the morning I walked on, ordering my servant to overtake me with my carriage; and he did so; but not till I had walked seven or eight miles.

Wednesday,14 December – I saw the Westminster scholars act the *Adelphi* of Terence, an entertainment not unworthy of a Christian. Oh how do these heathens shame us!

In the latter end of the month I took some pains in reading over Dr Young's *Night Thoughts*, leaving out the indifferent ones, correcting many of the rest, and explaining the hard words, in order to make that noble work more useful to all, and more intelligible to ordinary readers.

1769

'I have several times waived speaking about predestination or election – not that I am ashamed of the doctrine; because if it be indeed absurd, shocking, and unjust, the blame will not deservedly fall upon me, for I did not invent it, but upon the scriptures, where I am sure it is laid down in as plain terms, as that God created the heavens and the earth...'

'Every real conversion may be accounted miraculous, being no less than an immediate exertion of that power which made the heavens, and commanded the light to shine out of darkness.'

John Newton, from letters of 1775 and 1776

Sunday, 1 January – We met, as usual, at Spitalfields Chapel to renew our covenant with God. And we never do this without a blessing. Many were comforted, and many strengthened.

Monday, 9 January – I spent a comfortable and profitable hour with Mr Whitefield in calling to mind the former times, and the manner wherein God prepared us for a work which it had not then entered into our hearts to conceive.

Monday, 6 February – I spent an hour with a venerable woman, near ninety years of age, who retains her health, her senses, her understanding, and even her memory, to a good degree. In the last century she belonged to my grandfather Annesley's congregation, at whose house her father and she used to dine every Thursday; and she remembers to have frequently seen in his study, at the top of the house, with his window open, and without any fire, winter or summer. He lived seventy-seven years, and would probably have lived longer, had he not began water-drinking at seventy.

Friday, 17 February – I abridged Dr Watts' pretty *Treatise on the Passions*. His hundred and seventy-seven pages will make a useful tract of four-and-twenty. Why do persons who treat the same subjects with me, write so much larger books? Of many reasons, is not this the chief – we do not write with the same view? Their *principal end* is to get money; my *only one* to do good.

Sunday, 19 March – Elizabeth Oldham told me: I was saying to my little maid (always a serious and dutiful child, three years and a half old), 'Hannah, dost thou love God?' She eagerly answered, 'Yes, mammy, I do.' She added, 'I will go to God, I will go to God,' and leaned down and died.

Wednesday, 19 April – [Ireland] As it rained, I chose to preach in Mr McGeough's yard. The rain increasing, we retired into one of his buildings. This was the first time that I preached in a stable, and I believe more good was done by this than all the other sermons I have preached at Armagh.

Wednesday, 14 June – I preached in the market-house at Passage to as dull a congregation as I have seen. They would have been rude enough too, but that they stood in awe of Mr Freestone, who gave one and another, when they did not regard his signs, a stroke on the head with his stick. By this means the whole multitude was tolerably quiet, and many seemed much affected.

Tuesday, 20 June – [Aughrim] I spoke as plain as possibly I could to a money-loving people on 'God said unto him, Thou fool!' But I am afraid many of them are sermon-proof. Yet God has all power.

Sunday, 2 July – [Portarlington] I have not seen, in all the world, a people so easy to be convinced or persuaded as the Irish. What a pity that these excellent propensities should not always be applied to the most excellent purposes!

Thursday, 3 August – [Conference at Leeds] I mentioned the case of our brethren at New York, who had built the first Methodist preaching-house in America, and were in great want of money, but much more of preachers. Two of our preachers, Richard Boardman and Joseph Pilmoor, willingly offered themselves for the service; by whom we determined to send them fifty pounds, as a token of our brotherly love.

Wednesday, 16 August – I gave a second reading to that lively book, Mr Newton's *Account of his own Experience*. There is something very extraordinary therein, but one may account for it without a jot of Predestination. I doubt not but his was an answer to his mother's prayers.

Tuesday, 5 September – Last week I read over, as I rode, the great part of Homer's *Odyssey*. I always imagined it was, like Milton's *Paradise Regained* –

'The last faint effort of an expiring muse.'

But how was I mistaken! How far has Homer's later poem the pre-eminence over the former! It is not, indeed, without its blemishes; among which, perhaps, one might reckon his making Ulysses swim nine days and nine nights without sustenance; the incredible manner of his escape from Polyphemus and the introducing Minerva at every turn. But his numerous beauties make large amends for these. He likewise continually inserts the finest strokes of morality (which I cannot find in Virgil); on all occasions recommending the fear of God, with justice, mercy, and truth.

Wednesday, 20 September – [Bradford-on-Avon] The beasts of the people were tolerably quiet till I had nearly finished my sermon. They then lifted up their voice, especially one, called a gentleman, who had filled his pocket with rotten eggs; but, a young man coming unawares, clapped his hands on each side, and mashed them all at once. In an instant he was perfume all over; though it was not so sweet as balsam.

Tuesday, 17 October – Having appointed to preach in Oxford at ten, I was under some difficulty. I did not like to preach in the

Dissenting meeting-house; and I did not see how to avoid it. But the proprietors cut the knot for me by locking up the doors. So I preached in James Mears's garden.

Monday, 25 December (being *Christmas Day*) – We had such a congregation at four as I have not seen for many years. And from morning to evening we had abundant proof that God is visiting and redeeming his people.

Tuesday, 26 December – I read the letters from our preachers in America, informing us that God had begun a glorious work there; that both in New York and Philadelphia multitudes flock to hear; and that the society in each place already contains above a hundred members.

1770

'When I was much younger than I am now, I thought myself almost infallible: but I bless God, I know myself better now.'
John Wesley, letter to Lady Huntingdon, 1770

Saturday, 3 February – And on the following days, I read with much expectation a celebrated book – Rousseau upon Education. But how was I disappointed! Surely a more consummate coxcomb never saw the sun! How amazingly full of himself! He is a mere misanthrope; a cynic all over. So indeed is his brother-infidel, Voltaire; and wellnigh as great a coxcomb. But he hides both his doggedness and vanity a little better. The advices which are good are trite and common, and those which are really his own, are lighter than vanity itself. Such discoveries I always expect from those who are too wise to believe their Bibles.

Friday, 23 February – I was desired to hear Mr Leoni sing at the Jewish synagogue. I never before saw a Jewish congregation behave so decently. Indeed, the place itself is so solemn that it might strike an awe upon those who have any thought of God.

Sunday, 18 March – [Wednesbury] In the evening I preached a funeral sermon for Elizabeth Longmore; I think, the first witness of Christian Perfection whom God raised up in these parts. Her death was suitable to her life. She praised God with every breath till he took her to himself.

Thursday, 22 March – [between Wolverhampton and Manchester] In this journey, I observed a mistake that almost universally prevails; and I desire all travellers to take good notice of it, which

may save them both from trouble and danger. Near thirty years ago I was thinking, 'How is it that no horse ever stumbles while I am reading?' (History, poetry, and philosophy I commonly read on horseback, having other employment at other times.) No account can possibly be given but this: because then I throw the reins on his neck. I then set myself to observe: in riding above a hundred thousand miles, I scarce ever remember any horse (except two, that would fall head over heels any way) to fall, or make a considerable stumble, while I rode *with a slack rein*. To fancy, therefore, that a tight rein prevents stumbling is a capital
blunder.

Tuesday, 8 May – [Arbroath Abbey] I know nothing like it in all North Britain. I paced it, and found it a hundred yards long. Part of the west end, which is still standing, shows it was full as high as Westminster Abbey. The zealous Reformers, they told us, burnt this down. God deliver us from reforming mobs!

I have seen no town in Scotland which increases so fast, or which is built with so much common sense, as this. Every house has a garden; and thus both health and convenience are consulted.

Saturday, 16 June – [Whitby] I found our preacher, James Brownfield, had just set up for himself. The reasons he gave for leaving the Methodists were (1) that they went to church; (2) that they held Perfection. I earnestly desired our society to leave him to God, and say nothing about him, good or bad.

Sunday, 17 June – We had a poor sermon at church. However, I went again in the afternoon, remembering the words of Mr Philip Henry, 'If the preacher does not know his duty, I bless God that I know mine.'

Monday, 25 June – I preached in Tadcaster at noon, and at Pateley Bridge in the evening. It rained, as usual, all the time; but the congregation stood as still as the trees.

Monday, 8 October – I preached at Pensford and Shepton Mallet on my way to Wincanton, one of the dullest places in all the county. I preached on Death in the evening, and Hell in the morning.

Saturday, 10 November – I returned to London, and had the melancholy news of Mr Whitefield's death confirmed by his executors, who desired me to preach his funeral sermon on Sunday the 18th. In order to write this, I retired to Lewisham on Monday; and on Sunday went to the chapel in Tottenham Court Road. An immense multitude was gathered together from all corners of the town. I was at first afraid that a great part of the congregation would not be able to hear; but it pleased God so to strengthen my voice that even those at the door heard distinctly.

The time appointed for my beginning at the Tabernacle was half-hour after five, but it was quite filled at three; so I began at four. Oh that all may hear the voice of him with whom are the issues of life and death; and who so loudly, by this unexpected stroke, calls all his children to love one another.

1771

'O for heaven! Where we shall mistake, judge, and grieve one another no more.'

George Whitefield, letter to John Wesley from Philadelphia, 11 September 1747

Wednesday, 2 January – I preached in the evening, at Deptford, a kind of funeral sermon for Mr Whitefield. In every place I wish to show all possible respect to the memory of that great and good man.

Wednesday, 23 January – For what cause I know not to this day, [my wife] set out for Newcastle, purposing 'never to return.' *Non eam reliqui; non dimisi; non revocabo.* [I have not left her, I did not dismiss her, I will not recall her.]

Thursday, 14 February – I went through both the upper and lower rooms of the London Workhouse. It contains about a hundred children, who are in as good order as any private family; and the whole house is as clean from top to bottom, as any gentleman's needs be.

Saturday, 13 April – [Athlone] There is now no opposition either from rich or poor. The consequence of this is there is no zeal, while the people 'dwell at ease.' Oh what state upon earth is exempt from danger! Some perish by the storm, but far more by the calm.

Saturday, 18 May – [Limerick] I dined at Mr S–'s. Such another family I have not seen in the kingdom. He and Mrs – are made for each other. And their ten children are in such order as I have not seen for many years; indeed, never since I left my father's house.

Thursday, 20 June – [Castlecaulfield] As we were walking, a horse turned short and struck me on the small of my back. Had he been but an inch or two nearer I should not have travelled any farther. As it was, I was well again in a few days.

Friday, 6 September – I spent an hour among our children at Kingswood. How long shall we be constrained to weave Penelope's web? What is become of the wonderful work of grace which God wrought in them last September? It is gone! It is vanished away! Then we must begin again; and in due time we shall reap, if we faint not.

Tuesday, 15 October – [South Leigh] Here it was that I preached my first sermon, six-and-forty years ago. One man was in my present audience who heard it. Most of the rest are gone to their long home.

Thursday, 17 October – [Oxford] I preached in a room well filled with deeply attentive hearers, on part of the Sermon on the Mount, the noblest compendium of religion which is to be found even in the oracles of God.

Monday, 21 October – [Chatham] I preached to a crowded audience, ripe for all the promises of God. How good is it for fallen man to earn his food by the sweat of his brow! Everywhere we find the labouring part of mankind the readiest to receive the gospel.

Saturday, 21 October – I met an old friend, James Hutton, whom I had not seen for five-and-twenty years. I felt this made no difference; my heart was quite open; his seemed to be the same; and we conversed just as we did in 1738, when we met in Fetter Lane.

Monday, 30 December – At my brother's request, I sat again for my picture. This melancholy employment always reminds me of that natural reflection:

> Behold, what frailty we in man may see!
> His shadow is less given to change than he.

1772

'Unless the divine power has raised you up I see not how you can go through your glorious enterprise, in opposing that execrable villany which is the scandal of religion, of England, and of human nature. But, if God be for you, who can be against you? Go on, in the name of God, and in the power of his might, till even American slavery, the vilest that ever saw the sun, shall vanish before it.'

John Wesley, letter to William Wilberforce MP, 1791

Tuesday, 4 January – I spent an agreeable hour with Dr Stonehouse, the oldest acquaintance I now have. He is the greatest genius in little things that ever fell under my notice. Almost everything about him is of his own invention, either in whole or in part. Even his fire-screen, his lamps of various sorts, his inkhorn, his very save-all. I really believe, were he seriously to set about it, he could invent the best mouse-trap that ever was.

Saturday, 1 February – I found an increase of the work of God even in Southwark. Those who so furiously opposed us some years ago, as though they would have swallowed us up quick, are now crumbled into nothing.

Friday, 7 February – [Hampton Court] Of pictures I do not pretend to be a judge; but there is one, by Paul Reubens, which particularly struck me. It is Zacharias and Elizabeth, with John the Baptist two or three years old, coming to visit Mary, and our Lord sitting upon her knee. The passions are surprisingly expressed, even in the children; but I could not see either the decency or common sense of painting them stark naked.

Tuesday, 11 February – I casually took a volume of what is called *A Sentimental Journey through France and Italy*. *Sentimental*! what is that? It is not English; he might as well say *Continental*. And this nonsensical word (who would believe it?) is become a fashionable one! However, the book agrees full well with the title. For oddity, uncouthness and unlikeness to all the world beside, I suppose, the writer is without a rival.

Wednesday, 12 February – I read a very different book, published by an honest Quaker, on that execrable sum of all villanies, commonly called the Slave-trade. I read of nothing like it in the heathen world; and it infinitely exceeds, in every instance of barbarity, whatever Christian slaves suffer in Mahometan countries.

Friday, 14 February – I began to execute a design, which had long been in my thoughts, to print as accurate an edition of my *Works* as a bookseller would do. Surely I ought to be as exact for God's sake as he would be for money.

Friday, 21 February – I met several of my friends, who had begun a subscription to prevent my riding on horseback; which I cannot do quite so well since a hurt which I got some months ago.

Friday, 28 February – I opened the new preaching-house in Poplar. One might say, consecrated it; for the English law does not require, nay, does not allow, any other consecration of churches than by performing public service therein.

Wednesday, 25 March – [Congleton] None is now left to speak against the Methodists, except Mr Sambach, the curate. He earnestly labours to drive them from the Church, but they will not leave it yet. They both love her Liturgy and her doctrine, and know not where to find better.

Monday, 6 April – In the afternoon I drank tea at Adam Oldham's. But how was I shocked! The children that used to cling about me, and drink in every word, had been at a boarding-school. There they had unlearned all religion, and had learned pride, vanity, affectation, and whatever could guard them against the knowledge and love of God. Methodist parents, who would send your girls headlong to hell, send them to a fashionable boarding-school!

Sunday, 12 April – [Whitehaven] At five (who would imagine it?) we had wellnigh all the gentry of the town; and 'the power of the Lord was present to heal them'. The same power was present at the meeting of the children. I never, in all my life, was so affected with any part of Solomon's Song as while one of the girls was repeating it.

Tuesday, 28 April – [Perth] They did me an honour I never thought of – presented me with the freedom of the city.

Saturday, 23 May – [Alnwick] I preached in the town hall. What a difference between an English and a Scotch congregation! These judge themselves rather than the preacher; and their aim is, not only to know, but to love and obey.

Thursday, 4 June – [Weardale] I was a little surprised, in looking attentively upon them, to observe so many beautiful faces as I never saw before in one congregation; many of the children in particular, twelve or fourteen of whom (chiefly boys) sat full in my view. But I allow much more might be owing to grace than nature, to the heaven within, that shone outward.

In two respects this society has always been peculiarly remarkable: the one, they have been the most liberal in providing every thing needful for the preachers; the other, they have been particularly careful with regard to marriage. They have in general married with each other; and that not for the sake of money, but virtue.

It was observable, too, that their leaders were upright men, alive to God, and having an uncommon gift in prayer. This was increased by their continual exercise of it.

Last summer the work of God revived, and gradually increased till the end of November. Then God began to make bare his arm in an extraordinary manner. Those who were strangers to God felt a sword in their bones, constraining them to roar aloud. Those who knew God were filled with joy unspeakable, and were almost equally loud in praise and thanksgiving. The convictions that seized the unawakened were generally exceeding deep; so that their cries drowned every other voice, and no other means could be used than the speaking to the distressed, one by one, and encouraging them to lay hold on Christ. And this has not been in vain.

It was observed above that this work greatly resembled that at Everton.:

(1) in its unexpected beginning.

(2) in the swiftness of its progress.

(3) in the number of persons both convinced and converted.

(4) in the outward symptoms which have attended it. Many trembled exceedingly, many fell to the ground, many were violently convulsed, and many seemed to be in the agonies of death; and the far greater part cried with a loud and bitter cry.

(5) in most of the instruments whom God employed. These were plain, artless men, simple of heart, but without any remarkable gifts; who (almost literally) knew 'nothing save Jesus Christ, and him crucified.'

In other respects they were widely different.

Saturday, 6 June – [Sunderland] As we were concluding, an eminent backslider came strongly into my mind; and I broke out abruptly, 'Lord, is Saul also among the prophets? Is James Watson here? If he be, show thy power!' Down dropped James Watson like a stone, and began crying aloud for mercy.

Tuesday, 30 June – Calling at a little inn on the moors, I spoke a few words to an old man there, as my wife did to the women of the house.

Friday, 14 August – At the request of my old friend Howell Harris, I preached at Trevecca, and we found our hearts knit together as at the beginning. He said, 'I have borne with those pert, ignorant young men, vulgarly called students, till I cannot in conscience bear any longer.'

Friday, 21 August – [Haverfordwest] After dinner we hasted to the passage; but the watermen were not in haste to fetch us over, so I sat down on a convenient stone and finished the little tract I had in hand.

Tuesday, 27 October – [Norwich] Finding abundance of people were out of work, and consequently, in the utmost want (such a general decay of trade having hardly been known in the memory of man), I enforced, in the evening, 'Seek ye first the kingdom of God, and his righteousness; and all these things shall be added unto you.'

Monday, 2 November – [Bury St Edmunds] I preached to a little, cold company, on the thirteenth chapter of the first Epistle to the Corinthians. This love is the very thing they want; but they did not like to be told so. But I could not help that: I must declare just what I find in the Book.

Wednesday, 2 December – I preached at the new preaching-house in the parish of Bromley. In speaking severally to the members of the society, I was surprised at the openness and artlessness of the people. Such I should never have expected to find within ten miles of London.

1773

'Wherever I have been, I have found the bulk of mankind, Christian as well as heathen, deplorably ignorant, vicious, and miserable... Sin and pain are on every side.'
'Franky, are you out of your wits? Why are you not at Bristol?'

    John Wesley, letters, 1773; the second, to a local preacher, was the shortest he ever sent.

Monday, 4 January – I began revising my letters and papers. One of them was wrote above a hundred and fifty years ago (in 1619), I suppose by my grandfather's father, to her he was to marry in a few days. Several were wrote by my brothers and me when at school, many while we were at the University; abundantly testifying what was our aim from our youth up.

Thursday, 7 January – I called where a child was dying of the small-pox, and rescued her from death and the doctors. The next week I made an end of revising my letters; and I could not but make one remark – that for above these forty years, of all the friends who were once the most closely united, and afterwards separated from me, every one had separated himself! He left me, not I him.

Thursday, 13 May – [Ireland] We went on, through a most dreary country, to Galway; where, at the late survey, there were twenty thousand Papists and five hundred Protestants. But which of them are Christians, have the mind that was in Christ, and walk as he walked? And without this, how little does it avail whether they are called Protestants or Papists!

Saturday, 3 July – [Dublin] I sent to the commanding officer to desire leave to preach in the barracks; but he replied he would have no innovations. No: whoredom, drunkenness, cursing, and swearing for ever!

Thursday, 15 July – [Between Witney and London] I read over that strange book, *The Life of Sextus Quintus*; a hog-driver at first, then a monk, a priest, a bishop, a cardinal, a pope. He was certainly as great a genius, in his way, as any that ever lived. He did great things, and designed far greater; but death prevented the execution. And he had many excellent qualities; but was full as far from being a Christian as Henry VIII or Oliver Cromwell.

Wednesday, 21 July – We had our Quarterly Meeting at London, at which I was surprised to find that our income does not yet answer our expense. My private account I find still worse. I have laboured as much as many writers; and all my labour has gained me, in seventy years, a debt of five or six hundred pounds.

Sunday, 22 August – [Gwennap] The people both filled [the amphitheatre] and covered the ground round about to a considerable distance. So that, there must be above two-and-thirty thousand people; the largest assembly I ever preached to. Yet I found all could hear, even to the skirts of the congregation! Perhaps the first time that a man of seventy had been heard by thirty thousand persons at once!

Tuesday, 12 October – Between Northampton and Towcester we met with a great natural curiosity, the largest elm I ever saw; it was twenty-eight feet in circumference, six feet more than that which was some years ago in Magdalen College walks at Oxford.

Friday, 29 October – I had the satisfaction of dining with an old friend. I hope she meant all the kindness she professed. If she did not, it was her own loss.

Monday, 22 November – I set out for Sussex, and found abundance of people willing to hear the good word; at Rye in particular. And they do many things gladly; but they will not part with the accursed thing, smuggling. So I fear with regard to these our labour will be in vain.

Friday, 17 December – Meeting with a celebrated book, a volume of Captain Cook's *Voyages*, I sat down to read it with huge expectation. But how was I disappointed! I observed (1) things absolutely incredible; (2) things absolutely impossible. So that I cannot but rank this narrative with that of Robinson Crusoe.

1774

'I. Learn *these tunes* before you learn any others...

II. Sing them *exactly* as they are printed here...

III. Sing *all*. See that you join with the congregation as frequently as you can...

IV. Sing *lustily* and with a good courage. Beware of singing as if you were half dead, or half asleep.

V. Sing *modestly*. Do not bawl, so as to be heard above or distinct from the rest of the congregation...

VI. Sing *in time*: whatever time is sung, be sure to keep with it. Do not run before nor stay behind...

VII Above all sing *spiritually*. Have an eye to God in every word you sing. Aim at pleasing *him* more than yourself, or any other creature...'

John Wesley, *Directions for Singing*, 1761

Monday, 24 January – I was desired by Mrs Wright, of New York, to let her take my effigy in waxwork. She has that of Mr Whitefield and many others, but none of them, I think, comes up to a well-drawn picture.

Tuesday, 8 March – Coming to Chippenham, I was informed that the floods had made the road by Marshfield impassable. So I went round by Bath, and came to Bristol just as my brother was giving out the hymn, and in time to beseech a crowded audience not to receive 'the grace of God in vain.'

Tuesday, 29 March – [Newcastle-under-Lyme] Abundance of people were soon gathered together, who surprised me not a little by mistaking the tune, and striking up the march in *Judas*

Maccabeus. Many of them had admirable voices, and tolerable skill. But we had one jarring string: a drunken gentleman was a little noisy, till he was carried away.

Sunday, 17 April – [Halifax] While I was at dinner one came from Huddersfield to tell me the vicar was willing I should preach in the church. Dr Leigh lending me his servant and his horse, I set out immediately; and, riding fast, came into the church while the vicar was reading the Psalms. It was well the people had no notice of my preaching till I came into the town: they quickly filled the church. I did not spare them.

Friday, 13 May – [Glasgow] I preached, on the old Green, to a people the greatest part of whom *hear* much, *know* everything, and *feel* nothing.

Friday, 20 May – [Monydie] Oh what a difference there is between the English and Scotch method of burial! The English does honour to human nature, and even to the poor remains, that were once a temple of the Holy Ghost! But when I see in Scotland a coffin put into the earth, and covered up without a word spoken, it reminds me of what was spoken concerning Jehoiakim, 'He shall be buried with the burial of an ass!'

Tuesday, 28 June – This being the first day of my seventy-second year, I was considering, How is this, that I find just the same strength as I did thirty years ago? The grand cause is the good pleasure of God, who doeth whatsoever pleaseth him. The chief means are (1) my constantly rising at four for about fifty years; (2) my generally preaching at five in the morning – one of the most healthy exercises in the world; (3) my never travelling less, by sea or land, than four thousand five hundred miles in a year.

Thursday, 25 August – [Wales] Everywhere I heard the same account of the proceedings at Llancroyes. The Jumpers were first in the court, and afterwards in the house. Some of them leaped up many times, men and women, several feet from the ground; they clapped their hands with the utmost violence; they shook their heads; they distorted all their features; they threw their arms and legs to and fro, in all variety of postures. Meantime the person of the house was delighted above measure, and said, 'Now the power of God is come indeed.'

Thursday, 6 October – [Bristol] I met those of our society who had votes in the ensuing election, and advised them (1) to vote, without fee or reward, for the person they judged most worthy; (2) to speak no evil of the person they voted against; and (3) to take care their spirits were not sharpened against those that voted on the other side.

Sunday, 13 November – [London] After a day of much labour, at my usual time (half-past nine) I lay down to rest. I told my servants, 'I must rise at three, the Norwich coach setting out at four.' Hearing one of them knock, though sooner than I expected, I rose and dressed myself; but afterwards I found it was but half-hour past ten. While I was considering what to do I heard a confused sound of many voices below, and looking out towards the yard, I saw it was as light as day. A large deal-yard, at a very small distance from us, was all in a light fire, from which the north-west wind drove the flames directly upon the Foundery; and there was no probability of help, for no water could be found. Perceiving I could be of no use, I took my diary and my papers and retired to a friend's house. I had no fear, committing the matter into God's hands and knowing he would do whatever was best. Immediately the wind turned about to south-east, and our pump supplied the engines with abundance of water, so that in a little more than two hours all the danger was over.

Wednesday, 23 November – [Ely] Oh what want of common sense! Water covered the high-road for a mile and a half. I asked, 'How must foot-people come to the town?' 'Why, they must wade through.'

I took a walk to the cathedral, one of the most beautiful I have seen. The western tower is exceeding grand, and the nave of an amazing height.

Friday, 25 November – I set out in a one-horse chaise, the wind being high and cold enough. Much snow lay on the ground, and much fell as we crept along over the fen-banks.

Honest Mr Tubbs would needs walk and lead the horse through water and mud up to his mid-leg, smiling and saying, 'We fen-men do not mind a little dirt.' When we had gone about four miles, the road would not admit of a chaise. So I borrowed a horse and rode forward; but not far, for all the grounds were under water. Here, therefore, I procured a boat full twice as large as a kneading-trough. I was at one end, and a boy at the other, who paddled me safe to Earith. There Miss L– waited for me with another chaise, which brought me to St Ives.

No Methodist, I was told, had preached in this town: so I thought it high time to begin.

Sunday, 25 December – [London] I buried the body of Esther Grimaldi, who died in the full triumph of faith. During the twelve festival days we had the Lord's Supper daily; a little emblem of the Primitive Church.

1775

'(Dr Johnson said that) Wesley thought of religion only.
That cannot be said now, after the flagrant part which Mr
John Wesley took against our American brethren, when,
in his own name, he threw out amongst his enthusiastick
flock the very individual combustibles of Dr Johnson's
'Taxation no Tyranny'...
But I should think myself very unworthy, if I did not at the
same time acknowledge Mr John Wesley's merit, as a
veteran 'Soldier of Jesus Christ', who has, I do believe,
'turned many from darkness to light, and from the power
of Satan to the living God.'

James Boswell, *Journal of a Tour to the Hebrides*

Wednesday, 22 February – I had an opportunity of seeing Mr
Gordon's curious garden at Mile End, the like of which I
suppose is hardly to be found in England, if in Europe. One
thing in particular I learned here, the real nature of the
tea-tree.

Friday, 17 March – [Newcastle-under-Lyme] I was obliged to
preach abroad. One buffoon laboured much to interrupt; but,
as he was bawling, with his mouth wide open, some arch boys
gave him such a mouthful of dirt as quite satisfied him.

Sunday, 9 April – [Dublin] The good old Dean of St Patrick's
desired me to come within the rails and assist him at the Lord's
Supper. This was a means of removing much prejudice from
those who were zealous for the Church.

Wednesday, 26 April – [Waterford] The rain drove us into the preaching-house – the most foul, horrid, miserable hole which I have seen since I left England. The next day I got into the open air, and a large congregation attended.

Monday, 22 May – [near Castlebar] I spent two or three hours in one of the loveliest places, and with one of the loveliest families, in the kingdom. How willingly I could have accepted the invitation to spend a few days here! Nay, at present I must be about my Father's business; but I trust to meet them in a still lovelier place.

Monday, 29 May – [Ballyhaise] I spent an hour with that venerable old man, Colonel Newburgh. It does me good to converse with those who have just finished their course, and are quivering over the great gulf.

Thursday, 1 June – [Londonderry] I had so deep a hoarseness that my voice was almost gone. However, pounded garlick, applied to the soles of my feet, took it away before the morning.

Sunday, 4 June (being *Whit Sunday*) – The Bishop preached a judicious, useful sermon on the blasphemy of the Holy Ghost. He is both a good writer and a good speaker; and he celebrated the Lord's Supper with admirable solemnity.

Tuesday, 6 June – The Bishop invited me to dinner; and told me, 'I know you do not love our hours, and will therefore order dinner to be on the table between two and three o'clock.' We had a piece of boiled beef and an English pudding. This is true good-breeding.

Friday, 27 October – [Hanslope] In my way I looked over a volume of Dr Swift's *Letters*. Was ever such trash palmed upon the world under the name of a great man? More than half of what is contained in those sixteen volumes would be dear at twopence a volume.

Saturday, 11 November – I made some additions to the *Calm Address to our American Colonies*. Need any one ask from what motive this was wrote? Let him look round: England is in a flame –

a flame of malice and rage against the King, and almost all that are in authority under him. I labour to put out this flame. Ought not every true patriot to do the same?

Sunday, 12 November – I was desired to preach, in Bethnal Green church, a charity sermon for the widows and orphans of the soldiers that were killed in America. Knowing how many would seek occasion of offence, I wrote down my sermon.

1776

Tuesday, 2 January – Being pressed to pay a visit to our brethren at Bristol, some of whom had been a little unsettled by the patriots, so called, I set out early; but the roads were so heavy that I could not get thither till night. I came just time enough, not to see, but to bury, poor Mr Hall, my brother-in-law, who died on Wednesday morning; I trust, in peace, for God had given him deep repentance. Such another monument of divine mercy, considering how low he had fallen, and from what height of holiness, I have not seen, no, not in seventy years! It is enough, if, after all his wanderings, we meet again in Abraham's bosom.

Sunday, 14 January – In this and the following week I endeavoured to finish the *Concise History of England*. I am sensible it must give offence, as in many parts I am quite singular, particularly with regard to those greatly injured characters, Richard III and Mary Queen of Scots. But I must speak as I think, although still waiting for, and willing to receive, better information.

Sunday, 28 January – I was desired to preach a charity sermon in Allhallows Church, Lombard Street. In the year 1735, above forty years ago, I preached in this church, at the earnest request of the churchwardens, to a numerous congregation who came, like me, with an intent to hear Dr Heylyn. This was the first time that, having no notes about me, I preached extempore.

Friday, 1 March – As we cannot depend on having the Foundery long, we met to consult about building a new chapel. Our petition to the City for a piece of ground lies before their committee.

Thursday, 16 May – I attended an ordination at Arbroath. The service lasted about four hours; but it did not strike me. It was doubtless very grave; but I thought it was very dull.

Saturday, 18 May – I read over Dr Johnson's *Tour to the Western Isles*. It is a very curious book, wrote with admirable sense, and, I think, great fidelity; although, in some respects, he is thought to bear hard on the nation, which I am satisfied he never intended.

Wednesday, 3 July – I preached at York on the fashionable religion, vulgarly called morality; and showed at large, from the accounts given of it by its ablest patrons, that it is neither better nor worse than Atheism.

Thursday, 4 July – In the evening I showed the nature and necessity of Christian love: *agape*, vilely rendered *charity*, to confound poor English readers.

Friday, 2 August – [City Road, London] We made our first subscription toward building a new chapel, and at this and the two following meetings above a thousand pounds were cheerfully subscribed.

Tuesday, 6 August – Our Conference began, which we observed with fasting and prayer, as well for our own nation as for our brethren in America.

Sunday, 11 August – [Bristol] I found Mr Fletcher a little better, and proposed his taking a journey with me to Cornwall, nothing being so likely to restore his health as a journey of four or five hundred miles; but his physician would in no wise consent.

Wednesday, 14 August – [Launceston] Here I found the plain reason why the work of God had gained no ground in this circuit all the year. The preachers had given up the Methodist testimony. Either they did not speak of Perfection at all (the peculiar doctrine committed to our trust), or they spoke of it only in general terms, without urging the believers to 'go on unto perfection', and to expect it every moment. And wherever this is not earnestly done, the work of God does not prosper.

Monday, 2 September – I read over an ingenious tract, containing some observations which I never saw before. In particular, that if corn sells for twice as much now as it did at the time of the Revolution, it is in effect no dearer than it was then, because we have now twice as much money.

Tuesday, 31 December – We concluded the year with solemn praise to God for continuing his great work in our land. It has never been intermitted one year or one month since the year 1738, in which my brother and I began to preach that strange doctrine of salvation by faith.

1777

Thursday, 2 January – I began expounding the book of
Ecclesiastes. I never before had so clear a sight either of the
meaning or the beauties of it. Neither did I imagine that the
several parts of it were so connected together; all tending to
prove that grand truth – that there is no happiness out of God.

Wednesday, 15 January – I began visiting those of our society
who lived in Bethnal Green hamlet. Many of them I found in
such poverty as few can conceive without seeing it. Such another
scene I saw the next day. One poor man was just creeping out of
his sick-bed to his ragged wife and three little children, who were
more than half naked, and the very picture of famine; when, one
bringing in a loaf of bread, they all ran, seized upon it, and tore it
in pieces in an instant. Who would not rejoice that there is
another world?

Monday, 14 April – [Liverpool] Many large ships are now laid up
in the docks, which had been employed for many years in buying
or stealing poor Africans, and selling them in America for
slaves. The men-butchers have now nothing to do at this

laudable occupation. Since the American war broke out, there is no demand for human cattle. So the men of Africa, as well as Europe, may enjoy their native liberty.

Thursday, 17 April – I called upon Mr Barker at Little Leigh, just tottering over the great gulf. Being straitened for time I rode from thence to Chester. I had not for some years rode so far on horseback, but it did me no hurt. After preaching, I took chaise and came to Middlewich, a little before the Liverpool coach, in which I went on to London.

Monday, 21 April was the day appointed for laying the foundation of the new chapel. The rain befriended us much by keeping away thousands who purposed to be there. But there were still such multitudes that it was with great difficulty I got through them to lay the first stone. Upon this was a plate of brass, on which was engraved, 'This was laid by Mr John Wesley, on April [2]1, 1777.' Probably this will be seen no more by any human eye; but will remain there till the earth and the works thereof are burned up.

Monday, 28 April – At one I took coach, and on Wednesday evening preached at Newcastle-upon-Tyne. I love our brethren in the southern counties; but still I find few among them that have the spirit of our northern societies.

Saturday, 19 July – [Pembroke] We had the most elegant congregation I have seen since we came into Wales. Some came in dancing and laughing, as into a theatre; but their mood was quickly changed, and in a few minutes they were as serious as my subject – Death. I believe, if they do not take great care, they will remember it – for a week!

Friday, 1 August – [Bristol] I desired as many as could to join together in fasting and prayer, that God would restore the spirit of love and of a sound mind to the poor deluded rebels in America.

Tuesday, 5 August – Our yearly Conference began. I now particularly inquired, 'Have you reason to believe that the Methodists are a fallen people? Is there a decay or an increase in the work of God where you have been?' In most places the Methodists are still a poor, despised people, labouring under reproach, and many inconveniences. But they do not decrease in number; they continually increase; therefore, they are not a fallen people.

Thursday, 14 August – [London] I drew up proposals for *The Arminian Magazine*. Friday the 15th the committee for the building met, which is now ready for the roof. Hitherto God has helped us!

1778

'The first quarter of an hour of his sermon was addressed to his numerous female auditors on the absurdity of the enormous dressing of their heads.'

    Contemporary press report of the opening of the New Chapel, 1 November 1778

Wednesday, 21 January – [Shoreham] Mr Perronet, though in his eighty-fifth year, is still able to go through the whole Sunday service. How merciful is God to the poor people of Shoreham!

Monday, 2 February – This week I visited the society, and found a surprising difference in their worldly circumstances. Five or six years ago, one in three among the lower rank of people was out of employment. I did not now, after all the tragical outcries of want of trade that fill the nation, find one in ten out of business; nay, scarce one in twenty, even in Spitalfields.

Wednesday, 29 April – [Cork] Oh when will even the Methodists learn not to exaggerate? After all the pompous accounts I had had of the vast increase of the society, it is not increased at all; nay, it is a little smaller than it was three years ago. Many of the members are alive to God. But the smiling world hangs heavy upon them.

Tuesday, 1 September – [Tiverton] I heard a good man say long since: 'Once in seven years I burn all my sermons; for it is a shame if I cannot write better sermons now than I could seven years ago.' Whatever others can do, I really cannot. I may have read five or six hundred books more than I had then, and may know a little more history, or natural philosophy, than I did; but I am not sensible that this has made any essential addition to my knowledge in divinity. Forty years ago I preached every Christian doctrine which I preach now.

Monday, 14 September – [Bristol] I carefully examined whether there was any truth in the assertion that above a hundred in our society were concerned in unlawful distilling. The result was that I found two persons, and no more, that were concerned therein.

Saturday, 3 October – Visiting one at the poorhouse at Bristol, I was much moved to see such company of poor, maimed, halt, and blind, who seemed to have no one caring for their souls. So I appointed to be there the next day, and at two o'clock had all that could get out of bed, young and old, in the great hall. My heart was greatly enlarged toward them, and many blessed God for the consolation.

Wednesday, 14 October – I went on to Oxford, and, having an hour to spare, walked to Christ Church, for which I cannot but still retain a peculiar affection. What lovely mansions are these! What is wanting to make the inhabitants of them happy? That without which no rational creature can be happy – the experimental knowledge of God.

Sunday, 1 November, was the day appointed for opening the new chapel in the City Road. It is perfectly neat, but not fine; and contains far more people than the Foundery. I preached on part of Solomon's prayer at the dedication of the Temple; and both on the morning and afternoon (when I preached on the hundred forty and four thousand standing with the Lamb on Mount Zion), God was eminently present in the midst of the congregation.

Thursday, 5 December – [between Chatham and London] At Strood I chose to walk up the hill, leaving the coach to follow me. But it was in no great haste; it did not overtake me till I had walked above five miles. I cared not if it had been ten. The more I walk the sounder I sleep.

1779

Friday, 1 January – At length we have a house capable of containing the whole society. We met there this evening to renew our covenant with God.

Monday, 15 February – I went to Norwich in the stage-coach, with two very disagreeable companions, called a gentleman and gentlewoman, but equally ignorant, insolent, lewd, and profane.

Thursday, 25 March – I preached in the new house which Mr Fletcher has built in Madeley Wood. The people here exactly resemble those at Kingswood. But, for want of discipline, the immense pains which he has taken with them has not done the good which might have been expected. We took a view of the bridge, which is shortly to be thrown over the Severn. It is one arch, a hundred feet broad, fifty-two high, and eighteen wide; all of cast-iron, weighing many hundred tons.

Thursday, 22 April – I was a little surprised at a passage in Dr Smollett's *History of England*:

'Imposture and fanaticism still hang upon the skirts of religion. Weak minds were seduced by the delusions of a superstition, styled Methodism, raised upon the affectation of superior sanctity, and pretensions to divine illumination. Many thousands were infected with this enthusiasm by the endeavours of a few obscure preachers, such as Whitefield, and the two Wesleys.'

Friday, 30 April – [Harewood] There is too much sameness in all the great houses I have seen in England; two rows of large, square rooms, with costly beds, glasses, chairs and tables.

Wednesday, 3 July – I took a view of Flamborough Head. It is a huge rock, rising perpendicular from the sea to an immense height, which gives shelter to an innumerable multitude of sea-fowl of various kinds.

Friday, 23 July – I took coach for London. I was nobly attended; behind the coach were ten convicted felons, loudly blaspheming and rattling their chains; by my side sat a man with a loaded blunderbuss, and another upon the coach.

Sunday, 8 August – This was the last night which I spent at the Foundery. What hath God wrought there in one-and-forty years!

Saturday, 21 August – [Pembroke] Understanding that a large number of American prisoners were here, in the evening I took my stand over against the place where they were confined, so that they all could hear distinctly. Oh that God may set their souls at liberty!

Thursday, 23 September – [Bristol] One sat behind me who was one of our first masters at Kingswood. A little after he left the school he likewise left the society. Riches then flowed in upon him; with which, having no relations, Mr Spencer designed to do much good – after his death. 'But God said unto him, Thou fool!' Two hours after he died intestate, and left all his money to – be scrambled for!

Reader! if you have not done it already, make your will before you sleep!

Wednesday, 6 October – I preached in Winchester, where there are four thousand five hundred French prisoners. I was glad to find they have plenty of wholesome food, and are treated, in all respects, with great humanity.

Friday, 8 October – This night I lodged in the new house at London. How many more nights have I to spend there?

Tuesday, 7 December – [Rotherhithe] I preached in Redriff chapel, a cold, uncomfortable place, to a handful of people, who appeared to be just as much affected as the benches they sat upon.

1780

'I verily believe, I have as good a right to ordain as to administer the Lord's Supper. But I see abundance of reason why I should not use that right, unless I was turned out of the Church.'

John Wesley, letter to Charles, June 1780

Sunday, 2 January – We had the largest congregation at the renewal of our covenant with God which ever met upon the occasion; and we were thoroughly convinced that God was not departed from us. He never will, unless we first depart from him.

Tuesday, 18 January – Receiving more and more accounts of the increase of Popery, I believed it my duty to write a letter concerning it, which was afterwards inserted in the public papers. Many were grievously offended; but I cannot help it: I must follow my own conscience.

Wednesday, 12 April – [Rothwell] I inquired what was become of that lovely class of little girls, most of them believers, whom I met here a few years since. I found those of them that had pious parents remain to this day, but all of them whose parents did not fear God are gone back into the world.

Friday, 5 May – Notice having been given of my preaching at Nenthead, all the lead-miners that could got together, and I declared to them, 'All things are ready.' After riding over another enormous mountain, I preached at Gamblesby to a large congregation. The chief man of the town was formerly a local preacher, but now keeps his carriage. Has he increased in holiness as well as in wealth? If not, he has made a poor exchange.

Saturday, 20 May – [Edinburgh] I took one more walk through Holyrood House, the mansion of ancient kings. But how melancholy an appearance does it make now! The stately rooms are dirty as stables, the colours of the tapestry are quite faded, several of the pictures are cut and defaced. The roof of the royal chapel is fallen in, and the bones of James the Fifth and Lord Darnley are scattered about like those of sheep or oxen. Such is human greatness!

Thursday, 7 September – [Bath] I spent an hour with the children, the most diffcult part of our work.

Monday, 11 September – I wondered what had drawn such multitude of people together, till I learnt that one of the Members for the city had given an ox to be roasted whole. But their sport was sadly interrupted by heavy rain, which sent them home faster than they came, many of whom dropped in at our chapel, where I suppose they never had been before.

Saturday, 16 December – Having a second message from Lord George Gordon, earnestly desiring to see me, I wrote a line to Lord Stormont, who on Monday sent me a warrant. On Tuesday I spent an hour with him at his apartment in the Tower. Our conversation turned upon Popery and religion. He seemed to be well acquainted with the Bible, and had abundance of other books, enough to furnish a study. I cannot but hope his confinement will prove a lasting blessing to him.

Friday, 22 December – At the desire of some of my friends, I accompanied them to the British Museum. What an immense field is here for curiosity to range in! But what account will a man give to the Judge of quick and dead for a life spent in collecting all these?

Friday, 29 December – I saw the indictment of the Grand Jury against Lord George Gordon. What a shocking insult upon truth and common sense! But it is the usual *form*. Why will not the Parliament remove this scandal from our nation?

Saturday, 30 December – Waking between one and two in the morning, I observed a bright light shine upon the chapel. I easily concluded there was a fire near, probably in the adjoining timber yard. If so, I knew it would soon lay us in ashes. I first called all the family to prayer; then, going out, we found the fire about a hundred yards off, and had broke out while the wind was south. But a sailor cried out, 'Avast! Avast! the wind is turned in a moment!' So it did, while we were at prayer, and so drove the flame from us.

1781

'You cannot avoid being very frequently among elegant
men and women that are without God in the world. And as
your *business* rather than your *choice* calls you into the fire,
I trust that you will not be burnt; seeing he whom you desire
to serve is able to deliver you even out of the burning fiery
furnace.

I am, dear Charles, Your very affectionate Uncle.'
John Wesley, letter to his nephew Charles Wesley
junior, 9 September 1781

Tuesday, 23 January – [Dorking] I buried the remains of Mrs
Attersal, a lovely woman, snatched away in the bloom of youth.
I trust it will be a blessing to many, and to her husband in
particular.

Thursday, 25 January – I spent an agreeable hour at a concert of
my nephews. But I was a little out of my element among lords
and ladies. I love plain music and plain company best.

Thursday, 19 April – [between Shrewsbury and Worcester] I
took Broseley in my way, and thereby had a view of the iron
bridge over the Severn, I suppose the first and the only one in
Europe. It will not soon be imitated.

Tuesday, 1 May – [St David's] The cathedral has been a large
and stately fabric. But a great part of it is fallen down already,
and the rest is hastening into ruin: one blessed fruit (among
many) of the bishops residing at a distance from their see. Here
are the tombs and effigies of many ancient worthies, but the
zealous Cromwellians broke off their noses, hands, and feet.

What had the Tudors done to them? Why, they were progenitors of kings.

Wednesday, 30 May – I embarked on board the packet-boat for the Isle of Man.

Monday, 4 June – We came to Bishop's Court, where good Bishop Wilson resided near threescore years.

Wednesday, 6 June – [Peel] Mr Crook desired me to meet the singers. I was agreeably surprised. I have not heard better singing either at Bristol or London. Many have admirable voices; and they sing with good judgment. Who would have expected this in the Isle of Man?

Thursday, 7 June – I met our little body of preachers. They were two-and-twenty in all. I never saw in England so many stout, well-looking preachers together.

Friday, 8 June – Having now visited the island round, east, south, north, and west, I was thoroughly convinced that we have no such circuit as this, either in England, Scotland, or Ireland. Here are no Papists, no Dissenters of any kind, no Calvinists, no disputers. The natives are a plain, artless, simple people; unpolished, that is, unpolluted.

Sunday, 2 September – [Gwennap] I believe two or three and twenty thousand were present, and I believe God enabled me so to speak that even those who stood farthest off could hear distinctly. I think this is my *ne plus ultra* [high-water mark]. I shall scarce see a larger congregation till we meet in the air.

Friday, 7 September – [Kingswood] I made a particular inquiry into the management of the school. I found some of the rules had not been observed at all, particularly that of rising in the morning. Surely Satan has a peculiar spite at this school!

Friday, 12 October – I came to London, and was informed that my wife died on Monday. This evening she was buried, though I was not informed of it till a day or two after.

1782

'I say the pulpit...
Must stand acknowledged, while the world shall stand,
The most important and effectual guard,
Support, and ornament of Virtue's cause.
There stands the messenger of truth; there stands
The legate of the skies! – His theme divine,
His office sacred, his credentials clear.
By him the violated law speaks out
Its thunders; and by him, in strains as sweet
As angels use, the Gospel whispers peace.'
William Cowper, 'The Task', published 1784

Friday, 5 April – [Oldham] Being asked to visit a dying woman, I no sooner entered the room than both she and her companions were in such an emotion as I have seldom seen. Some laughed, some cried; all were so transported that they could hardly speak. Oh how much better is it to go to the poor than to the rich, and to the house of mourning than to the house of feasting!

Monday, 15 April – I saw an uncommon sight – the preaching-house at Wigan filled, yea, crowded! Perhaps God will cause fruit to spring up even in this desolate place.

Sunday, 5 May – One of my horses having been so thoroughly lamed at Otley that he died in three or four days, I purchased another; but, as it was his way to stand still when he pleased, I set out as soon as possible. When we had gone three miles, the chaise stuck fast. I walked for about a mile, and then borrowed a horse, which brought me to Birstall before the prayers were ended.

Friday, 31 May – As I lodged with Lady Maxwell at Saughton Hall (a good old mansion-house, three miles from Edinburgh), she desired me to give a short discourse to a few of her poor neighbours. I did so, on the story of Dives and Lazarus.

Friday, 2 August – We observed as a day of fasting and prayer for a blessing on the ensuing Conference; and, I believe God clothed his word with power in an uncommon manner throughout the week, so that, were it only on this account, the preachers, who came from all parts, found their labour was not in vain.

Sunday, 3 November – [Norwich] I preached at half-past two, and again in the evening; after which I requested them to go away in silence, without any one speaking to another. They took my advice; they went away in profound silence, so that no sound was heard but that of their feet.

Monday, 4 November – At five in the morning the congregation was exceeding large. That in the evening seemed so deeply affected that I hope Norwich will again lift up its head.

1783

Wednesday, 1 January – May I begin to live to-day!

Sunday, 19 January – I preached at St Thomas's Church in the afternoon and at St Swithin's in the evening. The tide is now turned; so that I have more invitations to preach in churches than I can accept of.

Friday, 21 February – We examined our yearly accounts, and found the money received (just answering the expense) was upwards of three thousand pounds a year. But that is nothing to me; what I receive of it yearly is neither more nor less than thirty pounds.

Saturday, 3 May – [Dublin] There was an ordination at St Patrick's. I admired the solemnity wherewith the Archbishop went through the service, but the vacant faces of the ordained showed how little they were affected thereby. In the evening multitudes met to renew their covenant with God. But here was no vacant face to be seen; for God was in the midst, and manifested himself to many.

Wednesday, 7 May – The packet still delaying, I exhorted a large congregation to take care how they built their house upon the sand; and then cheerfully commended them to the grace of God.

Friday, 23 May – I set out for Derby; but the smith had so effectually lamed one of my horses, that many told me he would never be able to travel more. I thought, 'Even this may be made matter of prayer': and set out cheerfully. The horse, instead of growing worse and worse, went better and better; and in the afternoon (after I had preached at Leek by the way) brought me safe to Derby.

Sunday, 25 May – I had an easy day's work, as Mr Bayley assisted me by reading prayers and delivering the wine at the Lord's Table.

Sunday, 1 June – I was refreshed by the very sight of the congregation at the new chapel. Monday the 2nd and the following days I employed in settling my business and preparing for my little excursion.

Wednesday, 11 June – I took coach with Mr Brackenbury, Broadbent, and Whitfield; and in the evening we reached Harwich. About nine in the morning we sailed; and at nine on Friday the 13th landed at Hellevoetsluis. Here we hired a coach for Brielle; at Brielle we took a boat to Rotterdam. We took a walk round the town, all as clean as a gentleman's parlour. Many of the houses are as high as those in the main street at Edinburgh, and the canals, running through the chief streets, make them convenient as well as pleasant, bringing the merchants' goods up to their doors. Stately trees grow on all their banks.

Saturday, 14 June – I had much conversation with the two English ministers, sensible, well-bred, serious men. These were very willing I should preach in their churches; but they thought it would be best for me to preach in the Episcopal church. In the evening we again took a walk and I observed the streets, the outside and inside of houses in every part, doors, windows, well-staircases, furniture, even floors, are kept so nicely clean that you cannot find a speck of dirt. The women and children (which I least of all expected) were in general the most beautiful I ever saw. This was wonderfully set off by their dress, which was plain and neat in the highest degree.

Sunday, 15 June – The Episcopal church is very elegant both without and within. The service began at half-past nine. Such a congregation had not often been there before. In the afternoon the church was so filled as it had not been for these fifty years. I preached on 'God hath given us eternal life; and this life is in his Son.'

Monday, 16 June – We set out for The Hague. By the way we saw a curiosity: the gallows near the canal, surrounded with a knot of beautiful trees! So the dying man will have one pleasant prospect here, whatever befalls him hereafter! When we came to The Hague we were not disappointed. It is beautiful beyond expression. Being invited to tea by Madam van Wassenaar, I waited upon her in the afternoon. She received us with that easy openness and affability which is almost peculiar to Christians and persons of quality. After tea I expounded the three first verses of the thirteenth of the first Epistle to the Corinthians. Captain M. interpreted, sentence by sentence.

Saturday, 21 June – Nothing is wanting but the power of religion to make Amsterdam a paradise.

Tuesday, 24 June – We took a view of the new workhouse, which stands on one side of the Plantations. It much resembles Shoreditch Workhouse; only it is considerably larger. We saw many of the poor people, all at work, knitting, spinning, picking work, or weaving. And the women in one room were all sewing. Many of these had been women of the town; for this is a Bridewell and workhouse in one. The head keeper was stalking to and fro, with a large silver-hilted sword by his side.

Wednesday, 26 June – We took boat for Haarlem. The great church here is a noble structure, equalled by few cathedrals in

England. The organ is the largest I ever saw, and is said to be the finest in Europe. Hence we went to Mr Van Kampen's, whose wife was convinced of sin and justified by reading Mr Whitefield's Sermons.

Here we were as at home. How entirely were we mistaken in the Hollanders, supposing them to be of a cold, phlegmatic, unfriendly temper! I have not met with a more warmly affectionate people in all Europe! No, not in Ireland!

Saturday, 28 June – I have this day lived fourscore years; and, by the mercy of God, my eyes are not waxed dim. And what little strength of body or mind I had thirty years since, just the same I have now.

Tuesday, 1 July – I called on as many as I could of my friends, and we parted with much affection. I can by no means regret either the trouble or expense which attended this little journey. It opened me a way into, as it were, a new world. But those with whom I conversed were of the same spirit with my friends in England.

Tuesday, 15 July – [Oxford] Walking through the city, I observed it swiftly improving in everything but religion.

Tuesday, 29 July – [Bristol] Our Conference began, at which two important points were considered: first, the case of Birstall House, and secondly, the state of Kingswood School.

With regard to the latter, we all agreed that either the school should cease or the rules of it be punctually observed, particularly that the children should never play, and that a master should always be present with them.

Tuesday, 5 August – Early in the morning I was seized with a most impetuous flux. In a few hours it was joined by a violent and almost continual cramp, first in my feet, legs, thighs, then in my side and my throat. The case being judged extreme, a grain and a half of opium was given me in three doses. This speedily stopped the cramp, but at the same time took away my speech, hearing, and power of motion, and locked me up from head to foot, so that I lay a mere log. I then sent for Dr Drummond, who from that time attended me twice a day.

Wednesday, 13 August – I took a vomit, which almost shook me to pieces; but, however, did me good.

Sunday the 17th, and all the following week, my fever gradually abated, and on Sunday the 24th I preached at the New Room morning and afternoon.

Wednesday, 3 September – I consulted the preachers how it was best to proceed with Birstall House.

Friday, 5 September – I met the nineteen trustees, and, after exhorting them to peace and love, said: 'All that I desire is that this house may be settled on the Methodist plan; and the same clause may be inserted in your Deed which is inserted in the Deed of the new chapel in London, viz. "In case the doctrine or practice of any preacher should, in the opinion of the major part of the trustees, be not conformable to Mr Wesley's *Sermons* and *Notes on the New Testament*, another preacher shall be sent within three months."' Five of the trustees were willing to accept of our first proposals; the rest were not.

Thursday, 18 December – I spent two hours with that great man, Dr Johnson, who is sinking into the grave by a gentle decay.

1784

'How easily are bishops made
  By man's or woman's whim!
Wesley his hands on Coke hath laid,
  But who laid hands on him?'
Charles Wesley, following Dr Coke's 'Ordination' by
John, 1 September 1784

Monday, 12 January – Desiring to help some that were in pressing want, but not having any money left, I believed it was not improper, in such a case, to desire help from God. A few hours after one from whom I expected nothing less put ten pounds into my hands.

Monday, 15 March – [Stroud] To my surprise, I found the morning preaching was given up, as also in the neighbouring places. If this be the case while I am alive, what must it be when I am gone? Give up this, and Methodism too will degenerate into a mere sect, only distinguished by some opinions and modes of worship.

Wednesday, 17 March – [Tewkesbury] I admired their teach-ableness. On my mentioning the impropriety of standing at prayer, and sitting while we were singing praise to God, they all took advice; kneeling while we prayed, and stood up while we sung psalms.

Saturday, 10 April – I preached to a huge congregation at Manchester, and to a far larger at ten in the morning, being Easter Day. It was supposed there were near a thousand communicants. But hitherto the Lord has helped me in this respect also; I have found no congregation which my voice could not command.

Friday, 16 April – In the evening we had a very uncommon congregation at Wigan. Only one gentlewoman behaved 'as she used to do at church' (so several afterwards informed me); talking all the time, though no one answered her!

Wednesday, 5 May – [Aberdeen] I talked with the preachers, and showed them the hurt it did both to them and the people for any one preacher to stay six or eight weeks together in one place. Neither can he find matter for preaching every morning and evening, nor will the people come to hear him. Hence he grows cold by lying in bed, and so do the people. Whereas, if he never stays more than a fortnight together in one place, he may find matter enough, and the people will gladly hear him.

Thursday, 13 May – [Elgin] We took a view of the poor remains of the once-magnificent cathedral. What barbarians must they have been who hastened the destruction of this beautiful pile by taking the lead off the roof!

Friday, 14 May – We saw, at a distance, the Duke of Gordon's new house, six hundred and fifty feet in front. Well might the Indian ask, 'Are you white men no bigger than we red men? Then why do you build such lofty houses?'

Saturday, 26 June – I rode to Epworth, which I still love beyond most places in the world. In the evening I besought all them that had been so highly favoured 'not to receive the grace of God in vain.'

Tuesday, 13 July – I went to Burnley, a place which had been tried for many years, but without effect. It seems the time was now come. High and low, rich and poor, now flocked together from all quarters; and all were eager to hear, except one man, who was the town-crier. He began to bawl amain, till his wife ran to him and literally stopped his noise: she seized him with one hand and clapped the other upon his mouth, so that he could not get out one word.

Sunday, 18 July – [Bingley] Before service I stepped into the Sunday school, which contains two hundred and forty children taught every Sunday by several masters, and superintended by the curate. So many children in one parish are restrained from open sin, and taught a little good manners, at least, as well as to read the Bible. I find these schools springing up wherever I go. Perhaps God may have a deeper end therein than men are aware of.

Friday, 13 August – [Carmarthen] After preaching, I advised all the audience to copy after the decent behaviour of the Hollanders in and after public worship. They all took my advice; none opened their lips till they came into the open air.

Tuesday, 31 August – [Bristol] Dr Coke, Mr Whatcoat, and Mr Vasey came down from London in order to embark for America.

Wednesday, 1 September – Being now clear in my own mind, I took a step which I had long weighed, and appointed Mr Whatcoat and Mr Vasey to go and serve the desolate sheep in America.

Sunday, 12 September – [Kingswood] I preached under the shade of that double row of trees which I planted about forty years ago. How little did any one then think that they would answer such an intention!

Tuesday, 21 November – After dinner we set out for Wrestlingworth, and having a skilful guide, who rode before the chaise and picked out the best way, we drove four miles in only three hours.

Monday, 12 December – [Hinxworth] I had the satisfaction of meeting Mr Simeon, Fellow of King's College, in Cambridge. He has spent some time with Mr Fletcher at Madeley, two kindred souls much resembling each other both in fervour of spirit and in the earnestness of their address. He gave me the pleasing information that there are three parish churches in Cambridge wherein true scriptural religion is preached, and several young gentlemen who are happy partakers of it.

1785

Saturday, 1 January – Whether this be the last or no, may it be
the best year of my life!

Tuesday, 4 January – At this season we usually distribute coals
and bread among the poor of the society. But I now considered
they wanted clothes as well as food. So on this and the four
following days I walked through the town and begged two
hundred pounds, in order to clothe them that needed it most.
But it was hard work, as most of the streets were filled with
melting snow, which often lay ankle deep; so that my feet were
steeped in snow-water nearly from morning till evening.

Tuesday, 25 January – I spent two or three hours in the House
of Lords. I had frequently heard that this was the most
venerable assembly in England. But how was I disappointed!
What is a lord but a sinner, born to die!

Sunday, 13 February – I met the single women, and exhorted
them to consider, to prize, and to improve the advantages they
enjoyed.

Thursday, 24 March – I was now considering how strangely the grain of mustard-seed, planted about fifty years ago, has grown up. It has spread through all Great Britain and Ireland; the Isle of Wight and the Isle of Man; then to America from the Leeward Islands, through the whole continent, into Canada and Newfoundland. And the societies, in all these parts, walk by one rule, knowing religion is holy tempers; and striving to worship God, not in form only, but likewise 'in spirit and in truth.'

Friday, 16 April – [Dublin] The number of children that are clearly converted to God is particularly remarkable. Thirteen or fourteen little maidens, in one class, are rejoicing in God their Saviour; and are as serious and stayed in their whole behaviour as if they were thirty or forty years old.

Friday, 13 May – [Kilfinnan] I took a survey of the Danish mount, the first I have seen surrounded with a triple ditch. Is it not strange that the Irish, as well as the Scots, should so soon have driven out those merciless robbers who defied all the strength of England for so long?

Saturday, 14 May – I found a far greater curiosity, a large Druidical temple. I judged by my eye that it was not less than a hundred yards in diameter; and it was, if I remember right, full entire as Stonehenge. How our ancestors could bring or even heave these enormous stones, what modern can comprehend?

Tuesday, 17 May – [Kilchreest] The house being full of genteel company, I was as out of my element, there being no room to talk upon the only subject which deserves the attention of a rational creature.

Monday, 23 May – After a long day's journey, I preached in the new court-house at Sligo, to far the worst congregation that I have seen since I came into the kingdom. Some (miscalled gentry) laughed and talked without fear or shame, till I openly reproved them; and the rabble were equally rude near the door.

Monday, 1 August – Having, with a few select friends, weighed the matter thoroughly, I yielded to their judgement, and set apart three of our well-tried preachers, John Pawson, Thomas Hanby, and Joseph Taylor, to minister in Scotland.

Thursday, 25 August – [Land's End] We clambered down the rocks, to the very edge of the water; and I cannot think but the sea has gained some hundred yards since I was here forty years ago.

Sunday, 4 September – [Bristol] Finding a report had been spread abroad that I was just going to leave the Church, to satisfy those that were grieved I openly declared that I had now no more thought of separating from the Church than I had forty years ago.

Wednesday, 7 September – [near Mells] Just as I began, a wasp, though unprovoked, stung me upon the lip. I was afraid it would swell, so as to hinder my speaking; but it did not. I spoke distinctly, near two hours in all; and was no worse for it.

Saturday, 22 October – [Norwich] I spoke home to an uncommonly large congregation, telling them, 'Of all the people I have seen in the kingdom, for between forty and fifty years, you have been the most fickle, and yet the most stubborn.' However, our labour has not been lost, for many have died in peace; and God is able to say to the residue of these dry bones, 'Live!'

Sunday, 13 November – I preached at Shoreditch church. The congregation was very numerous, and the collection unusually large.

Thursday, 22 December – [Highgate] Considering how magnificent a place this is, I do not wonder so little good has been done here. For what has religion to do with palaces?

1786

'Ah, lovely appearance of death!
  What sight upon earth is so fair?
Not all the gay pageants that breathe
  Can with a dead body compare.
With solemn delight I survey
  The corpse when the spirit is fled
In love with the beautiful clay,
  And longing to lie in its stead.'
Charles Wesley, from *Funeral Hymns*; sung at the
deathbed of Abigail Pilsworth, 28 June 1786

Tuesday, 24 January – I was desired to go and hear the King deliver his speech in the House of Lords. But how agreeably was I surprised! He pronounced every word with exact propriety. I much doubt whether there be any other King in Europe that is so just and natural a speaker.

Sunday, 19 February – I preached in Horsleydown church, where (to my no small surprise) no man, woman, or child seemed to know me either by face or by name! But before I had done many of the numerous congregation knew that God was there of a truth.

Monday, 27 February – [Newbury] I have not passed such a night for these forty years, my lodging-room being just as cold as the outward air. I could not sleep at all till three in the morning. I rose at four, and set out at five. But the snow which fell in the night lay so deep, it was with much difficulty we reached Chippenham. Taking fresh horses there, we pushed on to Bath.

Sunday, 23 April – [Bradford] Surely the people of this town are highly favoured, having both a vicar and a curate that preach the truth.

Tuesday, 27 June – [Belton] While I was preaching, three little children, whom their mother had left at dinner, straggled out, and got to the side of a well which was near the house. The youngest, leaning over, fell in. The others striving to pull it out, the board gave way; in consequence of which they all fell in together. The young one fell under the bucket, and stirred no more; the others held for a while by the side of the well, and then sunk into the water, where it was supposed they lay half an hour. On coming to tell me, I advised immediately to rub them with salt, and to breathe strongly into their mouths. They did so, but the young one was past help; the others in two or three hours were as well as ever.

Wednesday, 28 June – This morning, Abigail Pilsworth, aged fourteen, was born into the world of spirits. When we went into the room where her remains lay, we were surprised. A more beautiful corpse I never saw.

Thursday, 29 June – I took a cheerful leave of my affectionate friends at Epworth, leaving them much more alive than I found them.

Saturday, 1 July – [Sheffield] I spoke very plain to a crowded audience on 'Now it is high time to awake out of sleep.' One of the hearers wrote me a nameless letter upon it. But he could remember nothing of the sermon, but only that 'the rising early was good for the nerves!'

Tuesday, 4 July – I went to Wentworth House, the splendid seat of the late Marquis of Rockingham. He lately had forty thousand a year in England, and fifteen or twenty thousand in Ireland. And what has he now? Six foot of earth.

Thursday, 6 July – We went on in a lovely afternoon, and through a lovely country, to Nottingham. I preached to a numerous and well-behaved congregation. I love this people: there is something wonderfully pleasing, both in their spirit and their behaviour.

Saturday, 8 July – I walked through the General Hospital. I never saw one so well ordered. Neatness, decency, and common sense shine through the whole. I do not wonder that many of the patients recover.

[In August, Wesley paid a third visit to Holland.]

Friday, 15 September – I described what I take to be the chief besetting sins of Bristol – love of money and love of ease.

Tuesday, 26 September – I now applied myself to the writing of Mr Fletcher's *Life*. To this I dedicated all the time I could spare, till November, from five in the morning till eight at night. These are my studying hours; I cannot write longer in a day without hurting my eyes.

Tuesday, 3 October – [Sheerness] The preaching-house here is now finished, but by means never heard of. The building was undertaken a few months since by a little handful of men, without any probable means of finishing it; but God so moved the hearts of the people in the Dock that even those who did not pretend to any religion, carpenters, shipwrights, labourers, ran up, at all their vacant hours, and worked with all their might, without any pay. By this means a large, square house was soon elegantly finished; and it is the neatest building, next to the new chapel in London, of any in the south of England!

Tuesday, 24 October – [Deptford] I was vehemently importuned to order the Sunday service in our room at the same time with that of the church. It is easy to see that this would be a formal separation for the Church.

Wednesday, 25 October – I went to Brentford, but had little comfort there. The society is almost dwindled to nothing. What have we gained by separating from the Church here?

Sunday, 5 November – I buried the remains of John Cowmeadow, another martyr to loud and long preaching. To save his life, if possible, when he was half dead, I took him to travel with me. But it was too late.

Sunday, 3 December – I administered the Lord's Supper, and afterwards attended our parish church. Besides the little company that went with me, and the clerk and minister, I think we had five men and six women; and this is a Christian country!

Sunday, 31 December – I strongly exhorted all who had not done it already to settle their temporal affairs without delay. It is a strange madness which still possesses many, who put off from day to day, till death comes in an hour when they looked not for it.

1787

'And I also received an affectionate letter from Mr Wesley, and am truly sorry that the venerable man ever dipped into the politics of America.'

'I did not think it practical expediency to obey Mr Wesley, at three thousand miles' distance in all matters relative to church government.'

> From the Journal of Francis Asbury, pioneer leader of American Methodism.

Tuesday, 2 January – I went over to Deptford; but, it seemed, I was got into a den of lions. Most of the leading men of the society were mad for separating from the Church. I told them: 'If you are resolved, you may have your service in church hours; but, remember, from that time you will see my face no more.'

Wednesday, 21 March – [Gloucester] I had the satisfaction of spending an hour with the Bishop; a sensible, candid, and, I hope, pious man.

Thursday, 22 March – I preached at Tewkesbury to the largest congregation I have seen there for many years; and, in the evening, to our lovely and loving people at Worcester – plain, old, genuine Methodists.

Friday, 30 March – [Burslem] I had appointed to preach at five in the morning; but soon after four I was saluted by a concert of music, both vocal and instrumental, at our gate, making the air ring with a hymn to the tune of Judas Maccabeus. It was a good prelude. So I began almost half an hour before five; yet the house was crowded both above and below.

Sunday, 8 April (being *Easter Day*) – I preached in Bethesda, Mr Smyth's new chapel. Mr Smyth read prayers, and gave out the hymns, which were sung by fifteen or twenty fine singers; the rest of the congregation listening with much attention, and as much devotion, as they would have done to an opera. But is this Christian worship? Or ought it ever to be suffered in a Christian church?

Sunday, 22 April – I opened and applied that glorious text, 'The help that is done upon earth, he doeth it himself.' Is it not strange that this text, Psalm 74:12, is vanished out of the new translation of the Psalms?

Wednesday, 25 April – I once more visited my old friends at Tullamore. Have all the balloons in Europe done so much good as can counterbalance the harm which one of them did here a year or two ago? It took fire in its flight, and dropped it down on the thatched houses so fast that it was not possible to quench it till most of the town was burned down.

Thursday, 17 May – [Limerick] I met the stewards and leaders, and inquired into the rise of the late misunderstanding. The matter itself was nothing, but want of patience on both sides had swelled the mole-hill into a mountain. Oh how patient, how meek, how gentle toward all men ought a preacher, especially a Methodist, to be!

Every time I preached I found more and more hope that God will revive his work in this city. I know he will, if the prayer-meetings are restored.

Saturday, 9 June – [Antrim] The Presbyterian minister offered me the use of a large and commodious house. The Bible in the pulpit lying open, I chose for my discourse the words which first met my eye, namely, 'When they had nothing to pay, he frankly forgave them both.'

Tuesday, 19 June – We went on through horrible roads to Newry. I wonder any should be so stupid as to prefer the Irish roads to the English. The huge unbroken stones of which they are generally made are enough to break any carriage in pieces. No, there is nothing equal to good English gravel, both for horses, carriages, and travellers.

Tuesday, 26 June – We were agreeably surprised with the arrival of Dr Coke, who came from Philadelphia in nine-and-twenty days, and gave us a pleasing account of the work of God in America.

Thursday, 28 June – I had the pleasure of a conversation with Mr [John] Howard, I think one of the greatest men in Europe. Nothing but the mighty power of God can enable him to go through his difficult and dangerous employments.

Monday, 16 July – [Chester] I took a view of Mr Ryle's silk-mill, which keeps two hundred and fifty children in perpetual employment.

Friday, 27 July – [Bolton] Here are eight hundred poor children taught in our Sunday schools by about eighty masters. About a hundred of them are taught to sing; and they sang so true that, all singing together, there seemed to be but one voice.

Monday, 6 August – Having taken the whole coach for Birmingham, we set out at twelve o'clock, expecting to be there about five in the evening; but, having six persons within and eight without, the coach could not bear the burden, but broke down before three in the morning. But, having patched it together as well as we could, we went on to Congleton and got another. But in an hour or two this broke also, and one of the horses was so thoroughly tired that he could hardly set one foot before the other. After all these hindrances, we got to Birmingham just at seven. Finding a large congregation waiting, I stepped out of the coach into the house, and began preaching without delay; and such was the goodness of God that I found no more weariness when I had done than if I had rested all the day.

Friday, 10 August – [Southampton] I went to hear the famous musician that plays upon the glasses. By my appearing there (as I had foreseen), a heap of gentry attended in the evening; and I believe several of them did not come in vain.

Saturday, 3 November – I had a long conversation with Mr Clulow, on that execrable Act called the Conventicle Act. After consulting the Act of Toleration with that of the fourteenth of Queen Anne, we were both clearly convinced that it was the safest way to license all our chapels, and all our travelling preachers, not as Dissenters, but simply 'preachers of the gospel'.

Thursday, 15 November – Even at Poplar I found a remarkable revival of the work of God. I never saw the preaching-house so filled before; and the power of the Lord seemed to rest on many of the hearers.

Sunday, 18 November – We had, as usual, a large congregation and a comfortable opportunity at Spitalfields.

Friday, 30 November – I met the Committee, to consider the state of our temporal circumstances. We are still running backward. Some way must be found to make our income answer our expenses.

Sunday, 9 December – [London] I went down at half-hour past five, but found no preacher in the chapel, so I preached myself. Afterwards, inquiring why none of my family attended the morning preaching, they said it was because they sat up too late. I resolved to put a stop to this; and therefore ordered that (1) every one under my roof should go to bed at nine; (2) every one might attend the morning preaching. And so they have done ever since.

Tuesday, 18 December – I retired to Newington, and hid myself for almost three days.

Friday, 21 December – The Committee proposed (1) that families of men and women should sit together in both chapels; (2) that every one who took a pew should have it as his own.

Thus overthrowing, at one blow, the discipline which I have been establishing for fifty years!

Monday, 24 December – We had another meeting of the Committee, who, after a calm and loving consultation, judged it best (1) that the men and women should sit separate still; and (2) that none should claim any pew as his own.

1788

'1. Carry Dr Whitehead to him, whether my brother consents or no.

2. Get him out-door exercise if possible.

3. Let him be electrified – not shocked but filled with electric fire.

4. Inquire if he has made his will.'

John Wesley, note to the Rev. Samuel Bradburn about Charles Wesley, shortly before Charles's death in March 1788

Tuesday, 4 March – [Bristol] I gave notice of my design to preach on Thursday evening upon (what is now the general topic) Slavery. In consequence of this, on Thursday the house from end to end was filled with high and low, rich and poor. We set Friday apart as a day of fasting and prayer that God would remember those poor outcasts of men; and (what seems impossible with men, considering the wealth and power of their oppressors) make a way for them to escape, and break their chains in sunder.

[*Friday, 4 April* – Wesley heard news of his brother Charles's death on 29 March.]

Monday, 21 April – I went on, through miserable roads, to Blackburn.

Tuesday, 22 April – Through equally good roads we got on to Padiham. From hence we went through still more wonderful roads, to Haslingden. They were sufficient to lame any horses, and shake any carriage in pieces. – N.B. I will never attempt to travel these roads again till they are effectually mended!

Wednesday, 23 April – We hobbled on to Bury, through roads equally deplorable; but we met a lively congregation, which made us forget our labour.

Sunday, 18 May – [Glasgow] I subjoined a short account of Methodism, particularly insisting: There is no other religious society under heaven which requires nothing of men in order to their admission into it but a desire to save their souls. Look all round you: you cannot be admitted into the Church, or society of the Presbyterians, Anabaptists, Quakers, or any others, unless you hold the same opinions with them, and adhere to the same mode of worship.

The Methodists alone do not insist on your holding this or that opinion; but they think and let think. Neither do they impose any particular mode of worship. Here is our glorying; and a glorying peculiar to us; what society shares it with us?

Thursday, 5 June – [Weardale] Going out of my room, I missed a step, and fell forward, so that the edge of one of the stairs came a quarter of an inch above my right eye, exactly upon my eyelid. I put a little white paper upon it, which immediately stopped the bleeding, and preached without any inconvenience.

Wednesday, 11 June – [Stockton] I heard what was quite new to me, that it is now the custom, in all 'good' company, to give obscene healths, even though clergymen be present; one of whom, lately refusing to drink such a health, was put out of the room.

Wednesday, 11 June – I heard what was quite new to me, that it is now the custom, in all 'good' company, to give obscene healths, even though clergymen be present; one of whom, lately refusing to drink such a health, was put out of the room.

Saturday, 28 June – I this day enter on my eighty-fifth year. And what cause have I to praise God, as for a thousand spiritual blessings, so for bodily blessings also! It is true I am not so agile as I was in times past. I do not run or walk so fast as I did; my sight is a little decayed; my left eye is grown dim, and hardly serves me to read. I find likewise some decay in my memory in regard to names and things lately passed, but not at all with regard to what I have read or heard twenty, forty, or sixty years ago; neither do I find any decay in my hearing, smell, taste, or appetite (though I want but a third part of the food I did once); and I am not conscious of any decay in writing sermons, which I do as readily, and, I believe, as correctly, as ever.

To what cause can I impute this, that I am as I am? First, doubtless, to the power of God, fitting me for the work to which I am called, as long as he pleases to continue me therein; and, next, subordinately to this, to the prayers of his children.

May we not impute it, as inferior means:

1. To my constant exercise and change of air?

2. To my never having lost a night's sleep since I was born?

3. To my having sleep at command, so that whenever I feel myself almost worn out I call it, and it comes, day or night?

4. To my having constantly, for above sixty years, risen at four in the morning?

5. To my constant preaching at five in the morning for above fifty years?

Friday, 11 July – We set out early for Derby. About nine, within about a mile of the Peacock, suddenly the axletree of my chaise snapped asunder, and the carriage overturned. The horses stood still till Jenny Smith and I crept out at the fore-windows. The broken glass cut one of my gloves a little, but did us no other damage.

Sunday, 10 August – [London] I was engaged in a very unpleasing work, the discharge of an old servant. She had been my housekeeper at West Street for many years, and was one of the best I had had there; but her husband was so notorious a drunkard that I could not keep them in the house any longer. She received her dismissal in an excellent spirit, praying that God would bless us all.

I preached in the morning at West Street to a large congregation; the people in general do not expect that I shall remain a great while after my brother, and therefore they are willing to hear while they can.

Wednesday, 3 September – [Bristol] I made a little beginning of some account of my brother's life. Perhaps I may not live to finish it. Then let it fall into some better hands!

Saturday, 6 September – [Kingswood] I walked over to Hanham, and thence to Bristol. But my friends, more kind than wise, would scarce suffer it. It seemed so sad a thing to walk five or six miles! I am ashamed that a Methodist preacher, in tolerable health, should make any difficulty of this.

Monday, 6 October – [Lowestoft] When I came into the town it blew a storm, and many cried out, 'So it always does when he comes.' But it fell as suddenly as it rose; for God heard the prayer.

Wednesday, 10 December – [London] and the following days, I corrected my brother's posthumous poems.

Monday, 15 December – This week I dedicated to the reading over my brother's short poems on the Psalms, the four Gospels, and the Acts of the Apostles. Some are bad, some mean, and some most excellently good. They give the true sense of Scripture, always in good English, generally in good verse; many of them are equal to most, if not to any, he ever wrote; but some still savour of that poisonous mysticism with which we were both not a little tainted before we went to America.

Wednesday, 31 December – A numerous company concluded the old year with a very solemn watch-night. Hitherto God hath helped us, and we neither see nor feel any of those terrible judgements which it was said God would pour out upon the nation about the conclusion of the year.

1789

'Moore: Sir, do you mean to give a note of admission to the Holy Sacrament to Mr –?

Wesley: Yes, Henry; I have reason to believe that the report of his conduct is a mistake.

Moore: I have fully examined into it, sir, and I find it is no mistake; and if you give him a note, I shall not take the Sacrament myself.

Wesley: I would take the Sacrament if the devil himself were there.

Moore: And so would I, sir, but not if you gave him a note of admission!'

Conversation between John Wesley and the Rev. Henry Moore in the vestry of City Road Chapel, about a member alleged to have taken his family to the theatre: 1789

Thursday, 15 January – I retired to Camberwell, and carried on my Journal, probably as far as I shall live to write it.

Friday, 6 February – [London] I strongly insisted on St Paul's advice, 'Keep that which is committed to thy trust'; particularly the doctrine of Christian Perfection, which God has peculiarly entrusted to the Methodists.

Tuesday, 24 February – Mr Wilberforce called upon me, and we had an agreeable and useful conversation. What a blessing is it to Mr Pitt to have such a friend as this!

Wednesday, 18 March – [Tewkesbury] I was informed that one who, two or three years ago, had carried all his family to

America, in quest of golden mountains, had crept back again, being utterly beggared, and forced to leave his family behind.

Sunday, 28 June – [Dublin] This day I enter on my eighty-sixth year. I now find I grow old: (1) My sight is decayed, so that I cannot read a small print, unless in a strong light; (2) my strength is decayed, so that I walk much slower than I did some years since; (3) my memory of names is decayed, till I stop a little to recollect them.

Saturday, 8 August – [London] I chose a new person to prepare the *Arminian Magazine*, being obliged, however unwillingly, to drop Mr Olivers for only these two reasons: (1) The errata are unsufferable; I have borne them for these twelve years, but can bear them no longer. (2) Several pieces are inserted without my knowledge. I must try whether these things cannot be amended for the short residue of my life.

Saturday, 22 August – [Redruth] I preached to a huge multitude, from the steps of the market-house. I know not that ever I spent such a week in Cornwall before.

Sunday, 23 August – I preached there again in the morning, and in the evening at the amphitheatre, I suppose, for the last time; for my voice cannot now command the still increasing multitude.

Monday, 4 September – I spent an agreeable hour with Mr Ireland and Mr Romaine, at Brislington. I could willingly spend some time here; but I have none to spare.

Friday, 25 September – I spent an hour at Clare Hill with Mr Henderson; I believe the best physician for lunatics in England. But he could not save the life of his only son, who was probably taken to bring his father to God.

Sunday, 1 November – Being All Saints' Day, a day that I peculiarly love, I preached on Revelation 7:1; and we rejoiced with solemn joy.

Friday, 25 December (being *Christmas Day*) – We began the service in the new chapel at four o'clock, as usual; where I preached again in the evening, after having officiated in West Street at the common hour.

Saturday, 26 December – We had a very uncommon congregation in the evening, with a very uncommon blessing.

Sunday, 27 December – I preached in St Luke's, our parish church, in the afternoon, to a very numerous congregation, on 'The Spirit and the Bride say, "Come."' So are the tables turned, that I have now more invitations to preach in churches than I can accept of.

Monday, 28 December – I retired to Peckham, and at leisure hours read part of a very pretty trifle – the Life of Mrs Bellamy. Surely never did any, since John Dryden, study more –
'To make vice pleasing, and damnation shine.'
One anecdote concerning Mr Garrick, is curious. She says: 'When he was taking ship for England, a lady presented him with a parcel, which she desired him not to open till he was at sea. When he did he found Wesley's Hymns, which he immediately threw overboard.' I cannot believe it.

Thursday, 31 December – I preached at the new chapel; but, to avoid the cramp, went to bed at ten o'clock.

1790

'Oh my Lord, for God's sake, for Christ's sake, for pity's sake suffer the poor people to enjoy their religious as well as their civil liberty! I am on the brink of eternity! Perhaps so is your Lordship too! How soon may you also be called to give an account of your stewardship to the great Shepherd and Bishop of our souls! May he enable both you and me to do it with joy.'

John Wesley, letter to the Bishop of Lincoln, begging him to end his vendetta against Methodists, 26 June 1790

Friday, 1 January – I am now an old man, decayed from head to foot. My eyes are dim; my right hand shakes much; my mouth is hot and dry every morning; I have a lingering fever almost every day; my motion is weak and slow. However, blessed be God, I do not slack my labour. I can preach and write still.

Sunday, 3 January – I suppose near two thousand met at the new chapel to renew their covenant with God, a scriptural means of grace which is now almost everywhere forgotten except among the Methodists.

Tuesday, 16 February – I retired to Balham for a few days, in order to finish my sermons and put all my little things in order.

Friday, 26 March – [Madeley] I finished my sermon on the Wedding Garment; perhaps the last that I shall write. My eyes are now waxed dim; my natural force is abated. However, while I can, I would fain do a little for God before I drop in the dust.

In the evening I preached to a crowded audience at Salop, on 'Acquaint now thyself with him, and be at peace.'

Sunday, 4 April (being *Easter Day*) – [Manchester] I think we had about one thousand six hundred communicants. I preached, both morning and evening, without weariness.

Monday, 5 April – [Altrincham] I met with one of the most extraordinary phenomena that I ever saw, or heard of: Mr Sellers has in his yard a large Newfoundland dog and an old raven. These have fallen deeply in love with each other, and never desire to be apart. The bird has learned the bark of the dog, so that few can distinguish them. She is inconsolable when he goes out; and, if he stays out a day or two, she will get up all the bones and scraps she can, and hoard them up for him till he comes back.

Friday, 9 April – We went to Wigan, for many years proverbially called *wicked Wigan*. But it is not now what it was.

Friday, 28 May – We travelled through a delightful country, by Stirling and Kilsyth, to Glasgow. The congregation was miserably small; verifying what I had often heard before, that the Scots dearly love the word of the Lord – on the Lord's day. If I live to come again, I will take care to spend only the Lord's day at Glasgow.

Friday, 4 June – [Newcastle] In this and Kingswood house, were I to do my own will, I should choose to spend the short remainder of my days. But it cannot be; this is not my rest.

Tuesday, 8 June – I wrote a form for settling the preaching-houses without any superfluous words, which shall be used for the time to come, verbatim, for all the houses to which I contribute anything. I will no more encourage that villanous tautology of lawyers, which is the scandal of our nation.

Wednesday, 9 June – In the evening I took a solemn leave of this lovely people, perhaps never to see them more in this life, and set out early in the morning.

Monday, 28 June – This day I enter into my eighty-eighth year. For above eighty-six years I found none of the infirmities of old age. But last August I found almost a sudden change. My eyes were so dim that no glasses would help me. My strength likewise now quite forsook me, and probably will not return in this world.

Sunday, 29 August – [Bristol] Mr Baddiley being gone to the north, and Mr Collins being engaged elsewhere, I had none to assist in the service, and could not read the prayers myself; so I was obliged to shorten the service, which brought the prayers, sermon, and Lord's Supper within the compass of three hours.

Sunday, 5 September – [Bath] At ten we had more communicants than ever I saw here before. This day I cut off that vile custom of preaching three times a day by the same preacher to the same congregation; enough to weary out both the bodies and minds of the speaker as well as his hearers.

Wednesday, 13 October – [Norwich] The house would in no wise contain the congregation. How wonderfully is the tide turned! I am become an honourable man at Norwich. God has at length made our enemies to be at peace with us.

Friday, 22 October – We returned to London.

Sunday, 24 October – I explained, to a numerous congregation in Spitalfields church, 'the whole armour of God.' St Paul's, Shadwell, was still more crowded in the afternoon while I enforced that important truth, 'One thing is needful'; and I hope, many, even then, resolved to choose the better part.

WESLEY'S LAST DAYS

Wesley's last days

So ends the published Journal, at Spitalfields and Shadwell. John Wesley's diary, in note form, continued for another four months.

Meanwhile he continued to preach, even to travel. His devoted friend Elizabeth Ritchie was now caring for him, and by the beginning of February 1791 was very concerned for his health. He was at Leatherhead on 23 February for what proved to be his last sermon and the final entries in his diary. We owe to Miss Ritchie the full account of the following week, often printed at the end of the Journal.

From Monday February 28 he stayed mostly in bed, attended by Dr Whitehead and many more of his dearest friends. Isaac Watts' hymn, 'I'll praise my Maker while I've breath' was on his heart and lips, among several other psalms, hymns, and prayers. On Tuesday he twice cried out 'The best of all is, God is with us!', lifting up his arm and speaking 'with a holy triumph not to be expressed.'

Just before 10 o'clock on Wednesday morning, March 2, John Wesley died, after a final audible 'Farewell.'

1791

'I give the coins, and whatever else is found in the drawer of my bureau at London, to my dear granddaughters, Mary and Jane Smith...
I give £6 to be divided among the six poor men, named by the Assistant, who shall carry my body to the grave; for I particularly desire there may be no hearse, no coach, no escutcheons, no pomp, except the tears of them that loved me, and are following me to Abraham's bosom. I solemnly adjure my Executors, in the name of God, punctually to observe this... Lastly, I give to each of those travelling Preachers who shall remain in the Connexion six months after my decease, as a small token of my love, the eight volumes of Sermons.'

     from John Wesley's Last Will and Testament, made two years before his death.

'READER, if thou art constrained to bless the instrument GIVE GOD THE GLORY!'

     from the inscription on John Wesley's tomb

INDEXES

Bible Texts

Books and Publications

People

Places